Hemingway's Genders

Ernest Hemingway, his knee bandaged, with Sidney Franklin (holding
magazine) and other bullfighter friends on a swimming and paella party near
Madrid. See discussion of the unpublished essay "Portrait of Three or the
Paella," which begins on page 132.

Hemingway's Genders *Rereading the Hemingway Text*

Nancy R. Comley *and Robert Scholes*

Yale University Press   New Haven and London

Designed by Sonia L. Scanlon.
Set in Sabon type by Keystone Typesetting, Inc.,
Orwigsburg, Pennsylvania.
Printed in the United States of America by
Edwards Brothers, Ann Arbor, Michigan.

Library of Congress Cataloging-in-Publication Data
Comley, Nancy R.
Hemingway's Genders: Rereading the Hemingway
Text / Nancy R. Comley and Robert Scholes.
p. cm.
Includes bibliographical references (p.   ) and index.
ISBN 0-300-05967-1 (cloth)
      0-300-06464-0 (pbk.)
1. Hemingway, Ernest, 1899–1961—Criticism and
interpretation.   2. Masculinity (Psychology) in
literature.   3. Gender identity in literature.   4. Sex
role in literature.   I. Scholes, Robert E.   II. Title.
PS3515.E37Z823   1994
813'.52—dc20   93–49752
                  CIP

A catalogue record for this book is available from
the British Library.

The paper in this book meets the guidelines
for permanence and durability of the Committee on
Production Guidelines for Book Longevity of the
Council on Library Resources.

10 9 8 7 6 5 4 3 2

*We dedicate this book to the man who wrote the
following lines in his youth, perhaps not realizing
that they would one day apply to himself:*

And all the legends that he started in his life
Live on and prosper,
Unhampered now by his existence.

Contents

Preface

We believe that Ernest Hemingway remains an interesting writer because it is possible to read him in more than one way. We believe, even, that it is necessary to do so if his works are to maintain their place in the literary canon. Literary works survive over time because they continue to be part of a cultural conversation. They survive because succeeding generations of readers find their concerns represented in those texts and feel a need to discuss them with others, whether in casual speech or in more formal contexts like ours. To all who have read him in one way, as an embodiment of monolithic masculinity—and to all those who have resisted him on those grounds—we ask simply that you try reading him our way.

In this book we have attempted to read Hemingway by putting questions of gender ahead of all others. There are many indications in his writing that gender was a conscious preoccupation for Hemingway: in titles like *Men Without Women,* for instance. It is also the case, however, that current interest in these questions has established a frame of reference in which gender issues in all writing have become more visible and more interesting. We began working on this book with a broader focus in mind, but we found, during two years of intermittent research and writing, that questions of gender kept presenting themselves as the most fruitful questions to pose.

By *gender* we mean a system of sexual differentiation that is partly biological and partly cultural. This system is founded on a basic differentiation of humans into the categories male and female, but it extends into subcategories and cultural roles assigned to people and to literary characters in a given culture, and to categories of sexual practice as well. We are interested, for instance, in what a word like *girl* means in Hemingway's writing—or a word like *maricón*. Our assumption has been that sexual differentiations offer a productive and useful way into Hemingway's work. The results, which we offer in the following four chapters, will either justify or fail to justify that assumption.

One other feature of our approach that may need some explanation (not to say justification) is our concept of a Hemingway Text. Nietzsche kept wondering when people would get around to noticing that God was dead. Proponents of "The Death of the Author" seem to be experiencing a similar problem. We believe that the concept of an "author" is necessary for literary interpretation. But we have adopted what might be called a weak concept of authorship. A strong concept would require that all readings pass the test of referral to a fully realized intention on the part of an author: "No meanings where none intended," as Samuel Beckett once wrote in a passage we interpret as a joke. The weak concept of authorship that we have adopted is different from the strong one in a number of respects.

To begin with, we do not believe that authors are fully in control of their intentions or even fully aware of them. Nor do we believe that even those intentions of which they may be aware are likely to be fully realized in any particular written work. There is a sense in which it is correct to say that language and culture express themselves through the utterances of individuals. It is also, of course, the case that we have no direct access to an author called "Hemingway" and would not have it even if he were alive. We have only textual records of what he said, did, wrote, and so on. When we speak of the Hemingway Text we refer to a cultural matrix that we share with Hemingway, as this matrix appears when we imagine Ernest Hemingway at the center of it.

By putting Hemingway at the center, we mean that we will privilege his time and place over ours, that we will accept the best factual evidence of a biographical and bibliographical sort as decisive, and that, in short, we will make our imagined Hemingway as realistic or "true" as we can. In the center of our center lie Hemingway's words, because, after all, we are interested in him as a writer. However—and this is important—we will not be as concerned with the boundaries of individual works or with the difference between published and unpublished writings as some other critics have been. There are two reasons for this. One is a matter of our own critical methodology, our wish to understand his processes of composition. The other is a matter of the state of Hemingway's writing itself. He left an unusual amount of unpublished and unfinished work behind him, much of which has been edited and published by other people, which means that in many cases the difference between what he wrote and what was published cannot be attributed to Hemingway himself. He also sometimes took material that had been excised from one finished work and recycled it in another, or, conversely, borrowed from one unfinished manuscript something that could be used elsewhere. For instance, from our study of the manuscripts we conclude that he moved some items back and forth between *A Moveable Feast* and *The Garden of Eden*. And finally, we have found that excised portions of published stories often are more revealing about his thought processes than the more polished final versions.

Our critical method is directed not at the aesthetic dimension of Hemingway's work—neither his prose style nor the shape of his stories, admirable though these are—but at the ethical dimension. That is, we are concerned with the representation of human character in Hemingway's writing, especially with how characters are constructed along lines of gender and sexual behavior. Our notion of the Hemingway Text, then, puts Hemingway's writing and the facts of his life at the center and situates around this center various other cultural elements that must enter into any reading of that writing, starting with cultural objects we know Hemingway studied or encountered and extending to other cultural elements that throw light on Hemingway as a writer.

Our four essays were written to fit together, with each of them taking up the problem of gender from a different angle. In the first we concentrate on the notion of paternity in the myth of "Papa" and in Hemingway's writing. In the second we explore the repertory of female character types, beginning with maternity, deployed in the Hemingway Text. In the third we explore Hemingway's interest in transgressive sexuality, with emphasis on gender switching and miscegenation. And in the fourth we study male homosocial desire in stories of bullfighters and related writings. More could have been done with these topics, we are certain. These essays are not the last words on gender in the Hemingway Text. But a short book always has one virtue: its brevity—unless, short as it may be, it still seems too long. We hope our readers wish this one longer rather than shorter.

Acknowledgments

Parts of Chapters 1, 3, and 4 appeared earlier in the journals *Narrative, Novel,* and *differences,* respectively. We are grateful to the editors of each of them for permission to reprint. We are also grateful to the Hemingway Foundation for permission to quote from unpublished materials in the Hemingway Collection at the John F. Kennedy Library. We want to thank the curator of that collection, Megan Desnoyers; the assistant curator, Stephen Plotkin; and their assistants for all the help they have given us during many hours and whole days of research in those pleasant surroundings. We have also been helped by Samuel Streit, curator of Rare Books and Manuscripts at Brown University, and Russell Maylone at Northwestern University. Like all scholars, we owe librarians an immense debt, which we are eager to acknowledge.

Also, we are indebted to the many scholars whose work we have cited in this book. Among them, we'd like to give special mention here to Michael Reynolds and Paul Smith, to whose books we have turned regularly for assistance.

Finally, we are happy to give thanks here to our colleagues at Brown, Queens College of the City University of New York, the School of Criticism and Theory, Dartmouth College, the University of Wyoming, and Bates College for listening to us and arguing with us about Hemingway and his work.

1 Decoding Papa

"I wish my father wasn't such a damn fool."

"Everybody's father is a damn fool," Mike said.

—"Fathers and Sons," manuscript (K696)

What is a Papa? First of all, *Papa* is a word made of a single morpheme, repeated. In our language it denotes paternity, with connotations of patriarchy. It is a word with a rich and powerful cultural coding, but in the Hemingway Text it has a special meaning. Everybody knows two things about Ernest Hemingway: that he was called Papa and that he had a Code. These two things go together. That is, Papa was Papa because he had a Code, and the Code was the Code it was because it was the Code of a Papa. As Papa, Hemingway was an appropriately patriarchal figure, glorified by Malcolm Cowley in "A Portrait of Mister Papa" in *Life* (10 January 1949) and pilloried by Lillian Ross in her *New Yorker* profile of 13 May 1950. The image of Papa, though based on his private life, was exploited by Hemingway himself and by others as an icon, a marketing device that enhanced the salability of Hemingway as a commodity in magazines, in movies, and even in product endorsements—a tradition carried on by his children and grandchildren. The concept of a Hemingway Code played a similar role in the smaller sphere of literary criticism and reviewing. For both academic critics and journalistic reviewers, the Code was a form of intellectual packaging that made it simpler and easier to talk about Hemingway's writing. The notion of a single Code also, of course, always held out the possibility that some clever critic would crack this riddle and get to the heart of Hemingway's secret by thus decoding Papa.

Let us state unequivocally that this is not our intention. Recent biographical and critical studies of Hemingway—and, above all, his posthumously published writing and his unpublished manuscripts— have enabled us to get a much better idea of the complexities behind the mask of "Papa" and the network of codes behind the Code. We believe that it makes sense to see a writer's life and work as a network of codes that are cultural in origin but subject to selection, rejection, and modification by individuals. Creative achievements in any dimension of life—from politics and war to art and personal relations—are best understood in terms of an individual's ability to adopt and modify these cultural codes. We see Hemingway's achievements—his charismatic personality and his often fascinating prose—as signs of an exceptional will to textual power: an extraordinary strength in choosing and rejecting what his culture offered him, enabled in part by the abrupt displacements of his youth that forced him to compare the culture of Oak Park with the cultures of Europe and of war. On the other hand, we do not believe that Hemingway came close to achieving, in his life or in his work, a unified structure of thought and feeling that could be called the Hemingway Code any more than we believe that the name Papa designates an actual reality behind the commodity so easily marketed and satirized under that name. The code of baby talk gives us one kind of meaning for *Papa*. But the word has meanings in other codes, other contexts. Let us look at some:

1. papa papa papa
2. Pa-pa-pa-pa-pa-pa
3. Papa! Papa! Papa!

The syllable "pa" is easily formed by the human vocal apparatus. It is this ease that leads to its elemental function in a number of cultures. In English and some other modern languages, the repeated syllable becomes a childish name for Father. In ancient Greek it was a cry of pain. The quotations above are all from dramatic texts in which this repeated syllable occurs. As they stand, they are unintelligible, but they can be decoded. In decoding these Papas we will also be illustrating what we mean by the notion of a Hemingway Text. These examples originated in Western culture some distance from Hemingway and his world. In reaching out to them we are making an extravagant interpretive gesture, raising the question of whether they should be thought of as part of the Hemingway Text at all. We make such a gesture here, at the beginning, to claim our right to be extravagant in our textual interpretations. But we accept our responsibility to establish the connections between our most extravagant wanderings and those matters at the center of the Hemingway Text.

The first of the three quotations, transliterated from the Greek (παπα παπα παπα), is a cry of agony uttered by the hero Philoctetes in Sophocles' play (line 746, Laurentian manuscript). Edmund Wilson used this play as a metaphor for the modern artist in *The Wound and the Bow* (1941). Wilson included in that book a shrewd essay called "Hemingway: Gauge of Morale" in which he offered a balanced evaluation of Hemingway's strengths and weaknesses as a writer that is still a useful point of departure for readers and critics. In Sophocles' play the syllables "papa papa papa" are meaningless in themselves and are just a conventional way of representing pain that later editors have felt free to change and that translators usually reduce to something more dignified, like "ah" or "oh." For us, that cryptic encoding of what became Hemingway's nickname is simply a gift, a linguistic arrow pointing toward a major theme in Hemingway's work. *Philoctetes* is about the initiation into manhood of Achilles' son Neoptolemus, who has been ordered by Odysseus to dishonor himself and lie to Philoctetes. A prophet has said that Troy will not fall until Philoctetes brings the bow of Hercules into the fray on the side of the Greeks. But the Greeks, and Odysseus in particular, earned the undying enmity of Philoctetes by abandoning him on an uninhabited island after the bite of a serpent had given him a wound that smelled so bad and caused him to cry out so bitterly that no one could stand to be near him.

Ten years on the island in constant pain have not improved Philoctetes's disposition nor healed his wound. During these years he has been forced to use the bow and arrows given him by Hercules himself not in heroic action but to shoot birds and other animals for food. Odysseus, ordered to bring Philoctetes back with the indispensable weapon, resorts to trickery, enlisting Neoptolemus as his messenger. The boy is at first persuaded by Odysseus to lie, and with his lies he wins Philoctetes' friendship and obtains the bow—but remorse soon overwhelms him. He then tells Philoctetes the truth and returns the weapon to him, recovering his honor and finding his manhood by failing in his mission. The demigod Hercules then intervenes and puts things right. The play is about the conflict between Odysseus' code, in which the end justifies the means and winning is the only thing, and the code of Neoptolemus, who, like his father Achilles, puts honor first. It is a story about fathers and sons, about honor and expediency, and about coming of age. It is also, the scholars say, a play about Sophocles' own concerns over the loss of ancestral values in an Athens sick with pragmatism and selfishness. The play, written when Sophocles was almost ninety years old, is the playwright's *In Our Time.*

In short, it is a play as full of Hemingway themes as if Ernest had encoded them himself. Wilson was aware of this, observing in his condescending manner that the play was similar to but "much less crude in its subtlety" than "an underplayed affair of male loyalty in a story by Ernest Hemingway" (Wilson, 225). This judgment is itself crude in its intellectual snobbery, for the virtue of *Philoctetes* is strength, not subtlety, and an excellent case can be made for the subtlety and openness to interpretation of Hemingway's best writing. As a critic, however, Wilson was interested in Philoctetes as an archetypal figure or "parable of human character" (240) whom various writers had represented as the embodiment of some ultimate human truth. He thought that André Gide was on the right track in his play, *Philoctète,* in making Philoctetes a "literary man: at once a moralist and an artist, whose genius becomes purer and deeper in ratio to his isolation and outlawry" (236). But Wilson also believed that the fable of Philoctetes had a further implication not fully developed by Gide "but which must occur to the modern reader: the idea that genius and disease, like strength and mutilation, may be inextricably bound up together" (237). Wilson describes Neoptolemus as one who saves the alienated genius by "the recognition of his common humanity with the sick man . . . and thus cures him and sets him free, and saves the campaign as well" (242). Perhaps this is what Wilson meant by subtlety, but this interpretation is really irresponsible, because Sophocles makes it quite plain that Neoptolemus and Philoctetes are connected not by common humanity but by an aristocratic notion of virtue that sets them apart from the practical Odysseus and such common figures as Thersites, who is specifically linked with Odysseus in Sophocles' text. Wilson's reading of the play tells us more about Wilson himself than about Sophocles, and it suggests that he saw in the figure of Neoptolemus a version of Edmund Wilson as a literary critic who, by recognizing his common humanity with the diseased geniuses of modern literature, would rescue their works and make them socially productive.

We do not mean to sneer at Wilson, who was an exceptional literary critic, but we cannot accept his notion of criticism as therapy. We were led to *Philoctetes* by the cries of pain themselves, "papa papa," quoted by Gotthold Lessing in a discussion of representations of pain in poetry and painting (Lessing, 8). For those interested in Hemingway, the appearance of his nickname as a cry of pain is a lure that cannot be ignored. Following it led us back to Wilson's book and the established connection between Hemingway's work and Sophocles' play. It also led us to take greater note of the infected foot wound that laid up Hemingway during his honeymoon with Pauline Pfeiffer. Two of his finest

African stories are about the loss and recovery of honor ("The Short Happy Life of Francis Macomber") and about a hunter with a gangrenous leg dying painfully ("The Snows of Kilimanjaro"). Their connections to *Philoctetes* are eerily strong, though, so far as we know, Hemingway had not read the play. One suspects that Wilson used the play for the theme of *The Wound and the Bow* precisely because it worked so well for Hemingway and could, with ingenuity bordering on extravagance, be made to serve for such other figures as Dickens.

Wilson emphasized the psychic wounding or trauma that, in his view, constituted the origin of art, and he has been followed in this by Philip Young and other commentators on Hemingway. Hemingway himself hated this reduction of his achievement to a traumatic reflex. He was, however, well aware of a possible connection between physical trauma and mental activity, writing in *Death in the Afternoon* of Navarra as the place where "Loyola got his wound that made him think" (274–75), but he fiercely resisted the notion that his art emerged from some psychic wound. Our position on this vexed topic is that psychic wounds may indeed shape the concerns of artists, but what makes them artists instead of mere members of the walking wounded is what they can textualize, what they can draw within the bounds of textuality so that it can be brought to consciousness either by the writer or by readers. Looking for The Wound is like looking for The Code: it is an attempt to reduce a complex textual phenomenon to an excessively simple formula. It is to decode in a sense of the word that we are specifically rejecting.

Our method of decoding, involving as it does both extravagance and responsibility, carries its own risks and problems, of course. Specifically, we are suggesting that readers feel free to pursue textual lures and metaphorical trails that seem to lead away from any particular textual object in the hope that creative pursuit will result in a new approach to the original object—which may no longer seem the same. In particular, we recommend extending interpretation beyond the bounds of individual works and into the larger text of the cultural codes that are active in the thought of any writer as alert and sensitive as Ernest Hemingway. This means adopting more extravagant methods, such as the pursuit of textual lures and clues like the presence of the sound "pa pa" in the Greek text of Sophocles' play, which led us to a powerful Hemingway theme and to a whole school of critical interpretation stemming from Edmund Wilson's essay on Hemingway. We believe that such a procedure—which may seem irresponsible, if not bizarre—can lead to results at least as rewarding as those attained by more orthodox methods of interpretation. Not every trail will lead us to the wounded beast itself, of course, and it is up to the interpreter to avoid following spoors that lead only into brambles and briars and deserts of empty speculation. As readers, however, we may find that we are dealing with more than one trail, more than one beast. Having said this, we invite you to join us on the track of another Papa.

The second quotation ("Pa-pa-pa-pa-pa-pa") is from Mozart's *Magic Flute*. It is part of a duet between Papageno and his mate, Papagena, who are discussing their future procreative activities. Papageno is a genial figure of common humanity (a Mozartian Sancho Panza, and a humbler relative of Sophocles' Odysseus) who hunts and catches birds for the Queen of the Night. He comes upon a dead dragon and then brags that he has slain the beast, only to be exposed by the three women who have actually done the deed. They dispatched the dragon at the order of the Queen of the Night to protect Tamino, who, with his arrowless bow, fled before the dragon and fainted as the beast caught up with him. Our Papa Hemingway shared some qualities with both of these operatic males. He was a hunter who was not above exaggerating his exploits, and a handsome hero who sometimes needed and accepted

the help and protection of women. Occasionally he embraced the earthy
and self-serving code of Papageno, but more often took the high heroic
line of Tamino. Hemingway's world, like Tamino's, was inhabited by
perfectly lovely and devoted "girls," like Pamina, and nasty powerful
maternal figures (Mummies) like the Queen of the Night. Once again,
following a gratuitous trail of papas has led us to images and codes that
resonate powerfully with the texts of Hemingway's own life and art.

Our third quotation ("Papa! Papa! Papa!") comes from Richard
Strauss and Hugo von Hofmannsthal's decadent comedy *Der Rosen-
kavalier*. The words are uttered by a group of children falsely accusing
Baron Ochs (Ox) of having fathered them out of wedlock. Baron Ochs is
noble by birth, rustic by upbringing, and vulgar by nature—a sexual
predator and braggart who fancies himself supremely attractive and
hopes to marry a rich wife. In the opera his hopes are dashed when the
young bride is disgusted by him and falls in love with a youth (a role
always performed by a woman) who is sometimes disguised as a maid.
In her female disguise the youth attracts the erotic attentions of Baron
Ochs. This scenario of erotic displacement and gender confusion is one,
as we demonstrate in Chapter 3, to which Hemingway returned again
and again in his writing. He was himself, of course, in his life and in his
writing, an interesting mixture of civility and boorishness, enough so to
be characterized unfairly but perceptively by Wyndham Lewis as a
"bovine genius" ("The 'Dumb Ox,'" in *Men Without Art*, 36).

Papa as cry of pain, leading to initiation; Papa as sign of fecundity
and earthy happiness; Papa as sexual predator and dumb ox. Are these
our Papa? They are our Ernest Hemingway to a greater extent than any
public relations image or embodiment of a single Code can hope to be.
To pursue the meaning of *Papa* is to engender many papas, to find papa
written in many places and to write it ourselves, to tell more stories
about the morpheme "pa" and the figure textualized under that sign. In

the case of Hemingway it must also be a matter of looking at the way fatherhood itself is encoded in his writing as well as in his life, as, for example, in a story called "Fathers and Sons."

This is a story about Nicholas Adams, who is driving through a rural American countryside with his son sleeping beside him. He thinks of his father as he drives and of himself as his father's son. He is startled from these thoughts of himself as a son by his son's voice calling him Papa: "What was it like, Papa, when you were a little boy and used to hunt with the Indians?" (*CSS*, 375). This makes him think of all the things he cannot tell his son about, such as his first sexual experiences with an Ojibway girl:

> "You think we make a baby?" Trudy folded her brown legs together happily and rubbed against him. Something inside Nick had gone a long way away.
>
> "I don't think so," he said.
>
> "Make plenty baby what the hell."
>
> They heard Billy shoot.
>
> "I wonder if he got one?"
>
> "Don't care," said Trudy. (374)

We must remember that this scene is embedded in Nick's thought processes, though its dramatic form lends it an air of objective reporting. In Nick's memory, the answer to Trudy's question is a gunshot, which enables the young Nick to wonder aloud whether Trudy's brother has indeed killed a squirrel. Trudy's "don't care" is an eloquent comment on Nick's attempt to change the subject from procreation to hunting. This little scene is a node in the Hemingway Text in which two different ways of coding manhood encounter one another. In one code the dominant sign of manhood is the ability to hunt and kill game. The other code is sexual. In this code Trudy has made Nick a man by becoming his woman. In fact, Nick lent his gun to Billy in order to have some private time for his sexual encounter with Trudy, trading one sign of manhood for another—though neither sign is complete.

In the scene itself, the shot becomes Nick's excuse for breaking off an awkward conversation about paternity. Remembering the scene as he drives along with his son, the shot once again comes to Nick's aid, and the dead squirrel that Billy brings them replaces the "plenty baby" mentioned by Trudy. Nick gives that squirrel to Billy and Trudy. In terms of the hunting code, however, Nick is not yet a real hunter, being limited by his father to three shots a day. Nor, in the sexual code, is he yet a mature man, being unwilling to face the procreative consequences of his sexual pleasure. The problem of maturity is in fact a major focus of thought and feeling in the Hemingway Text. As we shall see, for Hemingway's male characters this problem is dominated by the possibility of there being a position between childhood and fatherhood. The desire for such a place animates much of Hemingway's most interesting writing—writing that is interesting precisely because in it this desired position is both proposed and contested in a variety of ways.

One of the ways this place is delineated is as something that lies between being a son and becoming a father. The birth of a son and that son's entry into manhood are two stages in the death of the father, two intimations of the father's death. This is why the answer to Trudy's suggestion of Papagenish behavior ("Make plenty baby what the hell") is not an embrace but a gunshot. Driving along with his sleeping son, and thinking of his own father, Nick Adams is led to an occasion (probably the first) in which he was confronted with the thought of his own potential fatherhood—and erases this thought with a gunshot. His father, as we learn, erased himself with a gunshot, and when he was a boy Nick had once thought of shooting his father himself.

This happened after he had refused to wear the underclothes of his father, insisting that they smelled even though they had been washed. They smelled, we would like to suggest, of paternity. Nick buried the unwanted garments and claimed to have lost them, whereupon his father whipped him for lying. "Afterward he had sat in the woodshed with the door open, his shotgun loaded and cocked, looking across at his father sitting on the screen porch reading the paper, and thought, 'I can blow him to hell. I can kill him.' Finally he felt his anger go out of him and he felt a little sick about it being the gun his father had given him. Then he had gone to the Indian camp, walking there in the dark to get rid of the smell" (375).

A Papa he may be, but Nick's thoughts in "Fathers and Sons" always return to himself as a son, just as thoughts of birth always seem to lead him to images of death. "Fathers and Sons" concludes with Nick's son wondering why they never go to pray at the grave of his grandfather and suggesting that Nick himself be buried at some convenient place and not "somewhere so that I can never go to pray at your tomb when you are dead." "We'll have to arrange it," Nick says dryly (377). One does not have to make a pilgrimage to Vienna to note that in the Hemingway Text fathers and sons seem always locked in a struggle to the death. A number of his finest early stories have a male protagonist—a proto-Papa—who resists fatherhood in one way or another.

In "Cat in the Rain," for instance, the young husband wants his wife to keep her hair "clipped close like a boy's" even though she is "tired of looking like a boy" (*CSS*, 131). The wife's desire to be a woman rather than a girl (or a boy) is signaled in many ways by the text, including her foregrounded wish to "have a kitty to sit on my lap" (131), which is reasonably read by many commentators as a sign of maternal longings. We would go further and suggest that this kitty is related to the squirrel—which was "bigger than a cat" (374)—brought to Nick and Trudy in "Fathers and Sons." The wife in "Cat in the Rain" may even be pregnant already: "Something felt very small and tight inside the girl" (130). But the husband, George, tries not to decode these messages, preferring to commune with the book he is reading. This is a subtle story in which the coding runs in more than one direction, however. At times the wife likes to feel small and important, like a little girl, as when the hotel keeper treats her in a fatherly manner.

A young man's resistance to fatherhood is more blatant in another story from *In Our Time*, "Cross-Country Snow." This story is set in the French part of Switzerland, near Montreux. It is partly a skiing idyll, in which two young American men enjoy the Alps and daydream about an endless ski trip around Switzerland and into Germany. The dark under-current of the idyll, however, is pregnancy. The waitress who serves the men in a little mountain inn is pregnant, unmarried, and unfriendly. The young men are very boyish. They say "gee" a lot. The sight of the pregnant waitress leads George to ask Nick if his wife, Helen, is going to have a baby. The conversation then goes this way:

> "Yes."
> "When?"
> "Late next summer."
> "Are you glad?"
> "Yes. Now." . . .
> "It's hell isn't it?"
> "No. Not exactly," Nick said. . . .
> "Maybe we'll never go skiing again, Nick," George said.
> "We've got to," Nick said. "It isn't worth while if you can't." (*CSS*, 146)

Pregnancy here signals the end of boyhood. George wants Nick to promise that they will go skiing together again, but Nick knows that "there isn't any good in promising" (147). Part of what is happening here is that the male bonding of the two young men is being hindered by bonds that society recognizes as stronger because they are reinforced by procreation. Nick tells George that the waitress is not married because "no girls get married around here until they get knocked up" (145). Pregnancy, then, interferes both with male bonding and with the desire to remain in that ideal place between boyhood and paternal manhood.

That place is also disputed territory in "Hills Like White Elephants," in which an American male at a Spanish railroad station is pressuring his "girl" to have an abortion. The young man says that he is "perfectly willing to go through with it if it means anything to you," adding, however, "I don't want anybody but you. I don't want anyone else" (*CSS,* 214). Anyone else could indicate another woman, but in this case the primary reference seems to be the possible child, who would break up their idyllic twosome, a life encoded in the labels on their bags, from "all the hotels where they had spent nights" (214), perhaps including the hotel in Rapallo that was the setting for "Cat in the Rain." In many of these early tales it seems as if what is being resisted is merely paternity itself and its attendant responsibilities, but there is also evidence in the larger Hemingway Text indicating that to father a son is to write your own death warrant.

Nick's memory (in "Fathers and Sons") of sitting with his loaded shotgun and thinking about blowing away his daddy concludes with the young Nick going to the Indian camp. In its immediate context this is quite plausible, but it also offers us a trail through the larger Hemingway Text to the story of that name, "Indian Camp." As Hemingway scholars know, this story was once preceded by some pages published in *The Nick Adams Stories* as "Three Shots." In this story the young Nick had just become aware of the possibility of his own death, stimulated by a hymn heard in church: "Some day the silver cord will break." This phrase led Nick to realize for the first time that "some day he must die. It made him feel quite sick. It was the first time he had ever realized that he himself would have to die sometime" (*NAS*, 14). Alone and afraid in the woods, he has made the signal of three rifle shots that would bring his father and uncle to the rescue. They come, talking of the boy as a coward and a liar, and he overhears them.

This story, with its focus on death, leads directly into "Indian Camp," in which birth and death are woven together in a manner typical of the Hemingway Text. In this story the boy Nick is present at the Indian camp as his father (who, like Ernest's, is a doctor) performs an emergency caesarian without anesthetic on an Indian woman. The baby is a son, born in the most painful way imaginable. The baby's father, who has been hurt in an accident, lies in the upper berth while his wife screams in agony below. He and the new baby constitute the second father-son pair in the story. For the doctor, the woman's "screams are not important. I don't hear them because they are not important" (*CSS*, 68). Nick is disturbed by them, however, and this links him with the Indian father, who is found after the operation is over to have slit his throat with a razor, apparently unable to bear his wife's suffering. In its powerful linkage of paternity and death, this story is thematically connected to those we have just discussed.

But there are other connections here that lead back toward the extravagant territory we were exploring earlier. The Indian has injured his foot, which has made him lame, like Oedipus ("swollen foot") and Philoctetes. The room in which he is lying is full of the sounds of agony, and it smells "very bad," like the island of Philoctetes. Philoctetes was the means of Neoptolemus' passage to manhood, and Oedipus, of course, killed his father. In this case Nick, who once contemplated killing his father but went to the Indian camp instead, encounters, in the story called "Indian Camp," a baby boy whose birth has just caused the death of his father. Unlike the classic Freudian scenario, in which the struggle between father and son would be over the body of the mother, in the Hemingway Text the struggle needs no third party because the very birth of the son threatens the life of the father. When Papa's sons were born he divorced their mothers and looked for another woman. And when he tried to write about being a good father in *Islands in the Stream,* he ended by killing off the sons. Papa, it seems, was always in flight from fatherhood because fatherhood was death. That is, he was as much an anti-Papa as he was a Papa. Textually, this meant retreating from paternity into the son's subject position. At the end of "Indian Camp" Nick has retreated to a more childlike state in which the breaking of the silver cord has been happily repressed: "In the early morning on the lake sitting in the stern of the boat with his father rowing, he felt quite sure that he would never die" (70).

The son's position, of course, is preeminently that of the narrator of "My Old Man," another early story about a father and son. Some critics believe that this story was written so much under the influence of Sherwood Anderson as to be peripheral in the Hemingway canon, but it is nonetheless important in the larger Hemingway Text. This story, told in the naïve voice of the son, is about a father who is a crooked jockey, exiled to European racetracks and blackballed even there. The death of the father in a horse race leads to the son's hearing his father referred to as a crook. A jockey friend—also, as we know, a crook—tells the boy not to pay attention to what he has heard, but the son knows so much he can scarcely continue to repress the facts. When told, "Your old man was one swell guy," he thinks, "I don't know. Seems like when they get started they don't leave a guy nothing" (*CSS,* 160).

Being left with nothing means not only losing one's father but losing one's innocence and youth as well. It means entering into the flux of time. In "My Old Man" the opposition to temporality is expressed by narration in the iterative mode: "I'd go ahead of him when we hit the road and I could run pretty good and I'd look around and he'd be jogging easy just behind me and after a little while I'd look around again and he'd begun to sweat. Sweating heavy and he'd just be dogging it along with his eyes on my back, but when he'd catch me looking at him he'd grin and say, 'Sweating plenty?' When my old man grinned, no-body could help but grin too. We'd keep right on running toward the mountains" (151). This is one narration of a repeated event, and in the Hemingway Text the iterative mode represents a grammatical triumph over temporality. The iterative can be used—as it is by D. H. Lawrence, for instance—to represent an enforced repetition that bars the movement of a character out into life, but in Hemingway's writing it usually encodes an idyllic pattern of living that time will inevitably destroy. In "Cross-Country Snow" and "Hills Like White Elephants" the force of temporality is encoded in a pregnancy that will end the iterative joys of youth. In "My Old Man" the death of the father signifies this same conclusion—a bitter end to a happier life. Pregnancy and the death of the father, linked in so many ways in the writings we have been reading, have similar meanings, signifying an involuntary and therefore discom-forting end of youth.

It would be easy to see these stories as advocating a rejection of maturity similar to that of Peter Pan. To make such a case, however, would require ignoring many instances in Hemingway's writing in which maturity is endorsed, and it would result in a Hemingway Text much less interesting than the one we are attempting to read. Even such an early work as "My Old Man" does not endorse the youthful narra-tor's deluded admiration of his father, though it offers the physical details of father and son's iterative round of life as highly attractive. Let us put it, then, that many of Hemingway's stories—and especially the early ones—pose the problem of how to attain maturity without pater-nity. They ask how one can cease to be a boy and become a man without

becoming a father like one's own father—and without losing the iterative joys of life. Behind this question, which Hemingway, like Freud,
posed almost exclusively in terms of a male subject position, can be
discerned dimly the same question posed from the female point of view:
How can one become a woman without also, fatally, becoming a
mother? If Hemingway's male figures are organized around a problem-
atic opposition of boyhood to fatherhood, his females may well be
deployed in a manner that is the shadow of this one, in which the space
between girlhood and motherhood is scarcely fit for human habitation.
As we shall see, however, this space in the Hemingway Text is occupied
by some very interesting figures.

2 Mothers, Nurses, Bitches, Girls, and Devils

"I'm your mother," she said. "I held you next to my heart when you were a tiny baby."
Krebs felt sick and vaguely nauseated.
"I know, Mummy," he said. "I'll try and be a good boy for you."
—"Soldier's Home"

If the male figures who populate the Hemingway Text emerge from some no-man's-land in the struggle between boyhood and paternity, what is the source of his textual females? The case we shall argue— sometimes explicitly, sometimes implicitly—is that, to a much greater extent than most writers of his stature, Hemingway worked all his life with a relatively simple repertory of male and female figures, modifying and individuating them with minimalist economy. The construction of this limited repertory company began for him with the family and its basic subject positions: father, mother, sister, brother. Hemingway's problem as a writer was to learn how to extend his range to figures who were not already given by the family romance. Specifically, it was a problem in the representation of the two figures denied or repressed by familial positioning and the incest taboo: the male and female who may be either the subjects or the objects of sexual desire.

In Chapter 4 we shall look at how a cultural formation like bullfight- ing enabled Hemingway to construct a range of adult male characters from a limited number of attributes or qualities. In this chapter, however, we start again with a familial figure—not Papa this time, but Mummy. Ernest Hemingway's mother was Grace Hall Hemingway. We can pic- ture young Ernest and his family in church of a Sunday, listening to their Congregationalist minister, the Reverend William E. Barton, proclaim- ing Christ's compatibility with free enterprise (Reynolds 1986, 11). In 1925 the son of this minister, Bruce Barton, would transform Jesus into a crackerjack salesman in his best-selling self-help book, *The Man Nobody Knows*. These matters are important because, within the Hemingway family, it was Grace who took the lead in the attempt to transform the Reverend Barton's capitalist Christianity into a code of conduct.

No one believed more strongly in Barton's Midwestern version of the Protestant ethic than Grace Hall Hemingway. As in so many American families, Mummy was primarily responsible for setting the moral tone while Papa, whose own moral stance was highly conservative, nonetheless performed some version of "lighting out for the territory." In the Hemingway household, Clarence instructed his son about hunting, fishing, and butchering. Grace did the heavy work on the Code. Her values, cast in the rhetoric of the Reverend Barton, pervade the letter she presented to her son, in whom she was not—and with good reason— well pleased, on the occasion of his twenty-first birthday, his nominal entry into manhood. She began by informing him that a mother's love is "like a bank" and that her children are each born "with a large and prosperous Bank Account, seemingly inexhaustible." During a child's first five years he draws continuously on this account as his mother acts almost as "a body slave to his every whim." Then, up to adolescence, the child continues to draw heavily for emotional support and guidance, making only "a few deposits of pennies" in the form of little services and "thank-yous." During the trying time of adolescence, the child turns on her, disregarding her advice, but she bears all this and hopes for the best. Such behavior, however, leaves the bank account "perilously low." Yet now that her child has reached manhood, Grace tells him, the bank is still paying out, a process that cannot continue:

The Account needs some deposits, by this time, some good sized ones in the way of gratitude and appreciation. Interest in Mother's ideas and affairs. Little comforts provided for the home. A desire to favor any of Mother's peculiar prejudices on no account to outrage her ideals. Flowers, fruit, candy, or something pretty to wear, brought home to Mother, with a kiss and a squeeze. The unfailing desire to make much of her feeble efforts, to praise her cooking, back up her little schemes. A real interest in hearing her sing, or play the piano, or tell the stories that she loves to tell—a surreptitious paying of bills, just to get them off Mother's mind.

A thoughtful remembrance and celebration of her birthday and Mother's day—the sweet letter, accompanying the gift or flowers, she treasures it, most of all. These are merely a few of the deposits, which keep the Account in good standing.

Many Mothers, I know, are receiving these and much more substantial gifts and returns from sons of less abilities, than my son.

Unless you, my son Ernest, come to yourself, cease your lazy loafing, and pleasure seeking,—borrowing with no thought of returning;—Stop trying to graft a living off anybody and everybody, spending all your earnings lavishly and wastefully on luxuries for yourself. Stop trading on your handsome face, to fool gullable little girls, and neglecting your duties to God and your Savior Jesus Christ, unless, in other words, you come into your manhood,—there is nothing before you but bankruptcy.

You have overdrawn.

Grace goes on to remind him that he was "born of a race of gentlemen . . . who were clean mouthed, chivalrous and generous" and that she expects him not to "disgrace their memory." In closing, she delivers her ultimatum: "Do not come back, until your tongue has learned not to insult and shame your Mother. When you have changed your ideas and aims in life you will find your Mother waiting to welcome you, whether it be in this world or the next,—loving you, and longing for your love" (K24, July 1920).

The position of Mummy, in the Hemingway family structure, was occupied by a female figure similar to Father Purdom in James Joyce's story "Grace," who offers a sermon on God as the great Accountant in the Sky and preaches in favor of befriending the Mammon of Iniquity.

Grace indeed. But Grace Hemingway is not, in the quoted letter, simply extending the Protestant ethic into a Banking Theory of Mother Love, she is also declaring her son bankrupt. In addition to this, as it happens, she is providing a model of how emotional qualities may be reduced to economic quantities—a formula her son would adapt to his own purposes in fiction and in life. But the maternal banker is only one position that Grace Hemingway sought to occupy in her son's emotional world. She also, like many other American mothers of her generation, wanted to be her son's "best girl." This stop (the *vox puella*?) is pulled out in her letter when she describes the sort of deposits she wants made in the love account: "Flowers, fruit, candy, or something pretty to wear, brought home to Mother, with a kiss and a squeeze." It is a tone that she had sounded two years earlier after receiving a letter in which Ernest announced (apparently as a joke) that he was about to be married.

On that occasion, after a letter in which she undertook to imagine how his new bride would receive him if he were to come home from the war crippled and disfigured, she wrote him a second letter in a softer vein: "My Darling Boy, Little Leicester came in this morning with a fist full of dandelions and that wonderful smile, for Mother. If I were an artist I would paint a picture entitled 'That Dandelion Smile.' It reminded me so of you, Ernest. It was only yesterday that you were Mother's little yellow headed laddie, and used to hug me and call me 'Silkey Sockey.' Don't forget, darling, that any girl who is worth while is worth waiting for and working for; and if she really loves you she will be willing to wait 'till you are a man, and able to take care of her" (K18, May 1918). The message is clear: I was your first best girl, and you are still my best beau. Even in this letter, however, tender emotions have a way of sliding into economic terms. The girl must be worth waiting for, and the wait must continue until Ernest is able to take care of her. Ernest, who was not serious about marrying in 1918, nonetheless did not wait until he could take care of a woman before marrying. Both his first two wives had bank accounts bigger than his and, to some extent, took care of him. This was an angle Grace had not foreseen, but the entanglement of emotional and economic perspectives was passed directly from Mummy to the son who became Papa. This had several results, one of which was Ernest's powerful drive to pay his own way— or to convince himself and others that he had done so. When he left his first wife he "repaid" her by giving her the royalties of *The Sun Also Rises*. This was a good and generous thing to do, but it was also a gesture interpretable in a code that makes emotional and economic things exchangeable.

In the Hemingway exchange system, to be a son is always to make recompense for the physical and mental pain one has caused one's mother. The scenes of childbirth in Hemingway's writing are vivid testimony to his sense of the price women paid in becoming mothers. He saw childbirth as a wretched exercise, fraught with pain and possibly resulting in death. Though the mother and the son survive a backwoods caesarian in "Indian Camp," the mother's screams of pain have quite literally killed her husband. The pain of motherhood can act at a distance, transmitting itself to those around it. In the interchapter following "Indian Camp," in the midst of the evacuation on the Karagatch road, "there was a woman having a kid with a young girl holding a blanket over her and crying. Scared sick looking at it" (*CSS*, 71). In "Indian Camp" Nick himself must have been scared sick, too, but there he was operating in the mode of little man (or Papa's "interne") and left any such feelings unexpressed until Hemingway found a use for them as a war correspondent. Another painful and prolonged labor concludes *A Farewell to Arms*, but this one, despite a last-minute caesarian, ends in death for both mother and son. Hemingway's many revisions of these pages reveal his indecision regarding the survival of the baby, but he finally decided to allow this son to pay his debt in full at birth and close his account (see Reynolds 1976).

Mothers, of course, have daughters as well as sons, but in the Hemingway Text the position of daughter is scarcely occupied. This is not hard to understand. Hemingway viewed the family configuration from the position of a son, which allowed only for figures defined as mother, father, brother, and sister. In his life, of course, Hemingway never had a daughter, but he wanted one so badly that this lack soured his last two marriages, if not all four of them. He compensated by writing daughter-lovers into some of his later works. But in his earlier fiction, mother, father, and son are the positions regularly deployed.

In the Adams family and its surrogates, neither Mother nor Father comes off very well, but Mother fares the worst. In "The Doctor and the Doctor's Wife" the doctor has been humiliated by having to back down from his challenge to an Indian woodcutter. Returning to his cottage, this father is not only forced to repress his anger, but he must listen to scriptural platitudes from his wife, speaking from her darkened bedroom, where she lies with her Christian Science publications on the bedside table. While she talks, the doctor cleans his shotgun ("He was very fond of it" [*CSS*, 75]) in his own bedroom, loading the magazine with shells and then pumping them out onto the bed in a grim mechano-sexual ritual. This loading and ejecting without firing is a powerful embodiment of the doctor's mental state, a displacement of repressed emotions in which the repression itself is not discharged but reenacted.

As he goes out for a walk his wife asks him to send Nick to her. When he finds Nick in the woods and tells him that his mother wants him, Nick says, "I want to go with you," and the two go off in search of black squirrels. Whether Nick has seen his father put to shame earlier is open to question; if he has, he still favors his father and the world they share in the woods. The interior, that dark space in which Mummy lurks, is to be avoided. This interior space is not simply that of the dark room but the entire house, for the houses of Nick's childhood belong to his mother. When the family is to move from one of these houses (her father's), the mother cleans out the attic where Nick, recalling the incident years later (in the story "Now I Lay Me"), remembers seeing the tin box holding "mother and father's wedding cake" and the "jars of snakes and other specimens" his father had collected in his youth. These specimens are judged unfit to be moved to the "new house designed and built by my mother" (CSS, 277). Nick remembers the snakes burning in a backyard fire, a sight critics like to associate with the emasculation of the father. The marriage cake, presumably, was not consigned to the flames. In the new house the process of purification continues. "About the house I remember how my mother was always cleaning things out and making a good clearance. One time when my father was away on a hunting trip she made a thorough cleaning out in the basement and burned everything that should not have been there" (278).

As Nick's father returns and notices the fire, his mother waits, smiling, on the porch. "I've been cleaning out the basement, dear," she says. Father has his shotgun again, but he hands it to Nick. Then, noticing just what it is that is being burned in this second backyard fire, he rakes out the blackened and chipped remains of the Indian artifacts he has collected over the years. "The best arrowheads went all to pieces," is all he says. The repetition of such cleanings and their attendant burnings suggests something more than mere housewifely earnestness. This is a ritual purification, a war not just on dirt but on objects that symbolize a domain antithetical to her own, a world of snakes and primitive weapons in which her husband has too great an investment to suit Mother Adams. A "good thorough cleaning out" was a phrase used by many a mother some decades ago when administering a dose of castor oil or some other purgative remedy for childish sulks or sicknesses. The body itself, with its irreducible primitive needs, is perhaps the enemy against which these rituals were directed. In the Hemingway Text, such episodes as these position Mummy not only against Papa but against everything natural and primitive, from snakes and arrowheads to bodily functions. In the second burning, the doctor's absence of anger—or rather its repression—is notable. He wraps up the charred fragments in a newspaper and carries them back into the house, presumably dirtier than ever, even though Mummy has made it clear that they do not belong there. In "Now I Lay Me" Nick doesn't comment on this recollection except to note that he prayed for both of the actors in that little domestic drama, but later Robert Jordan comments on his own similar background, thinking of his father as "just a coward. . . . Because if he wasn't a coward he would have stood up to that woman and not let her bully him" (*FWBT,* 339).

Nick's memories in "Now I Lay Me" take on added resonance in the full context of that story, since he is a soldier suffering from battle fatigue and is afraid to fall asleep, fearing his soul will leave his body. As the title suggests, Nick prays a lot during the night, and, as the title also suggests, in these prayers he regresses to a childish emotional state. "Now I Lay Me," a prayer taught to small children by well-meaning parents, is not especially comforting to someone in Nick's position:

Now I lay me down to sleep.
I pray the Lord my soul to keep.
If I should die before I wake,
I pray the Lord my soul to take.

This sweet prayer expresses precisely Nick's greatest fear, that his soul will indeed be taken if he falls asleep and that he will die. Nick's drowsy stream of consciousness, with its eerie obbligato of silkworms munching mulberry leaves in the dark, begins with fishing and the need to dig more worms for bait. When worms weren't available, he remembers, he would search out insects, beetles, and grubs, but he recalls too vividly the only time he tried to use a "neat and agile" salamander: "He had tiny feet that tried to hold on to the hook" (*CSS*, 277), like a soul, perhaps, in the hands of an indifferent God, or possibly like a husband with a domineering wife. The memory of this hooked and doomed creature, too humanoid for comfort, is followed a paragraph later by Nick's memories of his mother's houses and the burning of his father's treasures.

With Nick in the dark room is his orderly, John, who has a lot to say about his wife and kids in Chicago while urging Nick to get married. Nick thinks for a while about girls, but "finally they all blurred and all became rather the same." It was different with trout streams: "there was always something new about them" (*CSS*, 281–82). Later Nick thinks that John would be disappointed "if he knew that, so far, I have never married." To be married is to be hooked, and with his parents' marriage as his primary model, Nick can only assume that being hooked is painful—possibly involving the loss of one's soul.

Mummy as emotional banker, domineering spouse, and best girl were three maternal modes familiar to Ernest Hemingway as he grew up. All of them made him uneasy, and so did a fourth mode: Mummy as nurturer, as keeper of the breast upon which he was once utterly dependent. And if the odor of paternity was repugnant to him, the scent of maternity, of faintly sour breast milk, was far worse, as the reaction of Harold Krebs makes plain. In "Soldier's Home," Krebs, like the young Hemingway, is home from the war and feeling out of place. He is regarded by his parents as lacking ambition because he is not working, and thus not on his way to "being really a credit to the community." His mother gives him a little lecture on this topic, and when he doesn't respond she asks, "Don't you love your mother, dear boy?" He first answers no, but when this produces tears he is forced to say he didn't mean it and to beg her forgiveness. But this is not enough for her. She follows with her ultimate coercive weapon:

> "I'm your mother," she said. "I held you next to my heart when you were a tiny baby."
> Krebs felt sick and vaguely nauseated.
> "I know, Mummy," he said. "I'll try to be a good boy for you." (*CSS*, 116)

Mothers can drag a man into the complexities of the emotional swamp, a situation Krebs has sought to avoid. Shifting functions from best girl to nurturer, his mother reduces Krebs to the status of dependent infant in a sickening nightmare of the Mummy's Breast, from which he desperately wishes to escape. Grace Hemingway also liked to remind Ernest of his early years. On his nineteenth birthday, just after he was wounded, she wrote, "My Darling Boy, 19 years ago this morning at 7 A.M., I first knew that God had sent me a son. You were a mighty welcome laddie boy and it seems only yesterday that you were dependent upon me for everything" (K 21 July 1918). Krebs will go to Kansas City because the emotional cost of staying at home is much too high. Similarly, Grace Hemingway's maternal bookkeeping drove Ernest to seek work in Chicago.

This odd mixture of maternity and economics recurs in even odder circumstances in "The Mother of a Queen," in which Hemingway attempts to bury the mother problem by telling a story in which a mother remains unburied—on the public boneheap—because of the stinginess of her son. Since no red-blooded American boy would treat his Mummy this way, the job is given to a Mexican "queen" who fights bulls badly, in the manner attributed by Hemingway to a certain type of homosexual matador (a topic we shall explore in Chapter 4) who combines cowardice with stinginess. Paco, the queen of the title, refuses to pay (or support) people to whom he is obligated, such as Roger, the narrator, who lives with Paco and manages his affairs. Roger, insulted by Paco's willingness to give a "punk," a casual lover, more money than he will give Roger, leaves without what he is owed. Meeting Paco some time later in Madrid Roger tries to insult him with Hemingway's favorite Spanish taunt: "All I can say is that you never had a mother." But Paco is as handy with words as he is with the cape and turns the insult into a self-aggrandizing fiction: "My poor mother died when I was so young it seems as though I never had a mother. It's very sad" (CSS, 319). Roger concludes, "There's a queen for you. You can't touch them." There is no doubt that Paco is not presented as an admirable figure, but the psychic condition he has achieved is like that sought by Nick Adams in "Big Two-Hearted River." Nick is camping in the woods, alone in his tent, where "nothing could touch him" (CSS, 167). To reach this state Nick had to remove himself from society and damp down his thought processes, but Paco has achieved it as a modus vivendi.

Kenneth Lynn reads this story as a "revolting expression of a famous man's resentment at having to send a woman he hated a monthly allowance" (Lynn, 408), referring to money that Hemingway was sending his mother at that time (1933), but we see things as more complicated than that. Paco is clearly presented as a monster of egoism, so unnatural that Roger is twice impelled to ask "what kind of blood is it" that might account for such behavior. Paco himself is a master of romantic rhetoric, able to rationalize the consignment of his mother's remains to the boneheap in this manner: "Now I don't have to think about her buried in one place and be sad. Now she is all about me in the air, like the birds and flowers. Now she will always be with me" (CSS, 317). Nick Adams and Krebs, who are trying to free themselves of maternal ties with their own rituals and evasions, are clearly versions of Hemingway himself. But Paco?

Paco is a figure in the son-mother system of emotional banking in which Hemingway himself was clearly embroiled. But he is also a figure in a system of homosexual matadors that we shall explore in Chapter 4. Hemingway's fascination with these gay blades, which is as apparent as his attempts to distance himself from all forms of homosexuality, works to complicate any reading of this story. Paco's position is in certain respects like that of his author and like those of Krebs and Adams. To pay for perpetual care for his mother's grave (as his manager had done for Paco's father's grave) would be in effect to acknowledge a debt that could never be repaid. Further, to have the maternal body housed and protected in a grave would be always to recall the living body, in whose womb Paco had first been housed. By allowing that body to be dispersed Paco erases the evidence of his perpetual indebtedness and frees himself at last from the Mummy's curse. He does what no red-blooded American boy could bring himself to do, however many may have wished to. Hemingway offers him to us as a comic monster of ingratitude, one who is at least partly fashioned in his maker's image.

Mothers, Nurses, Whores The rejection of his own mother does not necessarily preclude a man's desire for certain qualities culturally defined as maternal. Agnes von Kurowsky, the nurse in Milan whom Hemingway wanted to marry, was seven years his senior. He fell hard for her, but she jilted him for an Italian officer whose mother subsequently forbade her son to marry someone she considered an American fortune hunter. A version of Hemingway's aborted romance became "A Very Short Story," written in 1923, soon after Hemingway had married Hadley Richardson, who was eight years older than he. Early drafts of the story are written in the first person, and the nurse's name is Ag. Later revisions transpose the voice to third person and change the nurse's name to Luz. The wounded soldier boy in this story enjoys both being mothered by Luz and embracing her in the very bed in which she has ministered to him. They have a joke about "friend or enema," but finally she does flush him, writing that "theirs had only been a boy and girl affair" and that she has in effect found a man. Agnes von Kurowsky's letter to Ernest, on which the fictional one is based, stresses the difference in their ages, as the fictional one does not.

> Now, after a couple of months away from you, I know that I am still very fond of you, but, it is more as a mother than a sweetheart.... So Kid (still Kid to me, & always will be) can you forgive me for unwittingly deceiving you? ... I am now & always will be too old, & that's the truth, & I can't get away from the fact that you're just a boy—a kid. (Villard and Nagel, 163)

Less than a year before, his mother had written him in a similar vein, telling him that he was too young (and too impecunious) to think of marrying (K 16 May 1918), following up that advice two days later with the letter in which she told him that "any girl who is worth while" would "wait till you are a man." Hearing the same advice from both Mummy and her nurturing surrogate must have been very bitter medicine for young Ernest. Friend or enema indeed. He responded by rewriting his unconsummated affair with Agnes von Kurowsky, giving his autobiographical character the sexual satisfaction he did not receive himself, making Luz's description of theirs as a boy and girl romance far less appropriate than the similar phrases in Agnes' letter. In "A Very Short Story," then, he would possess the desired maternal body and, on losing it to a detested Papa, take a childishly displaced revenge by causing his surrogate to contract gonorrhea from a salesgirl in a Chicago taxicab.

This experience of being jilted continued to haunt his imagination, however, demanding to be written yet one more time. If the first version was a farce, the next would be closer to tragedy; but it too would take its motivation from a man's desire to be loved by a kind, beautiful nurse-mother. In *A Farewell to Arms* young Ernest's role is played by an older and more sophisticated soldier, and the object of his affections, Catherine Barkley, is also provided with a past that serves to make her more interesting. She has suffered the loss of her lover in the war, and when she first meets Frederic Henry she uses him as a substitute for the dead man. He considers her "a little crazy" but finds their relationship better than going to the Villa Rossa, "where girls climbed all over you and put your cap on backwards as a sign of affection" (30). Before his next visit, he fantasizes about going to a hotel with Catherine, where she might "pretend that I was her boy that was killed" and grant Frederic the sexual favors she feels so guilty for having denied the other. As at the Villa Rossa, this would be a charade in which reality is kept at a distance, but in this case the emotional stakes would be higher.

His daydream becomes real after he has been wounded and is hospitalized in Milan. Here the wounded Frederic Henry plays a role in the fantasy that inspired Catherine Barkley to take up nursing in the first place: that her lover "might come to a hospital where I was, with a sabre cut, I suppose, and a bandage around his head" (20). When she appears in his room, looking "fresh and young and very beautiful," Frederic declares himself in love with her (91). In those days, a declaration of love was the minimum prerequisite for sexual intercourse between well-bred people. Knowing this, Frederic plays the love card to win a trick for his desire, which is heightened by his knowledge that Catherine is a virgin. Afterward she says, "Now do you believe I love you?" (92), having played the sex card to win a trick for love, bestowing the good girl's greatest treasure, which is given only when she is sure she's in love and believes that her young man is in love with her. His reaction—"The wildness was gone and I felt finer than I had ever felt" (92)—is indicative of that selfish state of male postcoital satiation that Hemingway understands so well and has represented so effectively in "Up in Michigan," in which the boorish male falls asleep snoring on top of Liz, and in "Summer People," in which Nick, his mind "working very hard and clear" after sex with Kate, says, "I'm hungry," which leads to fried chicken and cherry pie. Later, alone in bed, he prays for Kate and others, and "to be a great writer" (CSS, 503).

Catherine Barkley seems to be aware of the predominantly physical basis of Frederic Henry's "love," for, on the morning of her operation, as she performs her professional tasks of making him "clean inside and out," she questions him about the behavior of whores, coming to understand the rules of that game as one in which the whore "says just what he wants her to." Her questions are not idle, for she is exploring a new role for herself as a sexual partner. Thus she vows to "do what you want and then I'll be a great success" (FTA, 105). When he asks her to come to bed with him again and she agrees, he will no longer be her dead soldier-lover, but she will be his live nurse-whore. She offers herself, saying, "There isn't any me any more. Just what you want" (106).

Such apparent compliance and self-erasure have seemed appalling to many readers (though some male critics have found Catherine an ideal woman), but it is possible to read this episode in a slightly different way. We might, for instance, see Catherine not as erasing herself so much as assuming a role in a game of sex and love that allows her to transfer her affections to a man other than her dead fiancé. She assumes the role of whore as a means of escaping profoundly restrictive cultural codes— those of her social code, which require of her a chastity suitable to a grieving widow honoring her husband's memory, and those of her chosen profession, which forbid sexual relations between military nurses and their charges. As a "bad girl," she can learn to enjoy illicit sex in stolen moments. Switching back to her role as nurse, she becomes the ministering angel, the mother-Madonna, the body slave, thus enacting a primal male fantasy of modern culture that Frederic Henry, supine on his bed of pain and pleasure, amply equipped with wine and brandy, is in the ideal position to enjoy.

As Klaus Theweleit points out, "one of the pervasive male fantasies in our society concerns sexual relations with nurses. . . . It is that staple food on which, for example, Hemingway's [*A Farewell to Arms*] feeds. Equally well known is the fact that nurses refuse to conform to the images of them projected in male fantasies. . . . When all is said and done, the patient doesn't desire the nurse as a person, but as an incarnation of the caring mother, the nonerotic sister. Indeed, that may be why nurses are called 'sister' in so many countries" (126–27).

Where soldiers are concerned, the hospital situation is "highly conducive to that fantasized (non)love situation" because a person's wound "usually impedes his lovemaking ability." And, with his individual rights taken away, the soldier is in effect "reduced to the status of a child" and thus focuses his "needs for mother-child and sibling relations onto the sister-nurses" (Theweleit, 127). As a Red Cross nurse, Agnes von Kurowsky was "forbidden to carry on serious romances, even to be alone with a gentleman caller." Henry Villard, who was hospitalized in the room next to Hemingway's when he was in the same condition as Frederic Henry, concurs with Agnes' statement that a hospital affair such as that described in the novel "was totally implausible" (Villard and Nagel, 42).

But what a delicious fantasy, what a safe kind of regression to a time before one must confront the realities of an adult world. In *A Farewell to Arms*, Frederic Henry's childish status is reiterated throughout. His roommate Rinaldi's favorite epithet for him is Baby, and the priest and Catherine, among others, call him a good boy or urge him to be one. There are echoes here of Agnes von Kurowsky's pet names for Ernest, as found in her letters to him: Kid, Bambino, my boy, or Maestro Antico—

"the inversion of the same concept" (Villard and Nagel, 243). But this is the fantasy of a sexualized Oedipal child who desires the mother-sister-nurse. In the "real world" of the novel the characters enact the fantasy of the author. This fantasy does not end with Frederic Henry's recuperation and his return to the more adult world of the war, for his desire is always to return to the waiting Catherine, the faithful and loving mother-mistress. He is the hungry child who would devour his mother, and Catherine willingly abdicates from what little self she has to give herself over to his desires. Together they try to establish a world of their own, a world of oneness, as they move further from society into a life centered in the womblike protection of a Swiss featherbed.

Catherine knows, however, that they have done something wrong, because their sexual pleasure, however innocent they think it, has resulted in pregnancy. She resists marriage, knowing that it would result in separation, for (according to Red Cross rules) a woman cannot be both nurse (sister) and wife. Though Catherine is not worried about her pregnancy, Frederic Henry is, and when she announces it and tells him that she will look after the details of going away and having the baby, *he* is the one who says, "You always feel trapped biologically" (*FTA*, 139). But it is she who is trapped, and she will die in labor, because how else can the story end? Frederic Henry, the child-man, cannot be expected to share his mother-lover with a real baby. Thus, in the logic of the narrative, Catherine's determination to have the baby is her death warrant. Mother and child must go, and they do, erasing all vestiges of motherhood. Frederic survives, but, as Hemingway noted on an unpublished manuscript page of the novel, "the position of the survivor of a great calamity is seldom admirable" (Reynolds 1976, 60). The great calamity in this case is not so much war or death as love itself. As Hemingway observed in *Death in the Afternoon,* "If two people love each other there can be no happy end to it" (122). Whether or not this view is true for the world, it was true for Hemingway in the sense that his best writing was energized by precisely that view of human relations. When he forgot it, his work suffered.

Bitches, Girls, and Women In the 1930s Hemingway was occupied creatively with the Spanish Civil War, with Africa and the wealthy who hunted there, and with Key West and the wealthy who frequented it. Many of the women who populated the Hemingway Text during that era were drawn from a social formula for the "rich bitch," with Margot Macomber, who is a bitch married to a rich man, as the central exemplar of this type. As the label suggests, this is a group of women defined by a special combination of sex and money. The women in this phase of Hemingway's writing are for the most part more sexually aggressive than the men. They seem to exist solely for sex and the power that goes with it and to have few other interests. In this sense they may be seen as a reflection of the author's own problems with such strong and active women as his mother and his new love of that period, Martha Gellhorn. Hemingway was attracted to Gellhorn because of her appearance: she was long-legged, blonde, and very attractive. She was also adventurous, intelligent, and a competitive and talented writer who took her work seriously—and thus was a challenge to Hemingway. As a kind of revenge, Gellhorn is caricatured as Dorothy Bridges, the vapid Bryn Mawr girl in *The Fifth Column* who just can't understand a man's commitment to his cause.

In *To Have and Have Not,* Hemingway wove the story of Harry Morgan's misadventures against a background of the lives of the tourists and yachtsmen in Key West, setting up, as the title suggests, a contrast between the lives of the rich and the poor. With two of the female characters in this book—have-not Marie Morgan and have-a-lot Dorothy Hollis—Hemingway experimented with Molly Bloomish interior monologues as a means of showing that women, however different their backgrounds, have in common an insatiable desire for sex. Marie lies in bed thinking postcoital thoughts of how she "could do that all night if a man was built that way" (115), while on a yacht, Dorothy, denied sex because her boyfriend, Eddie, is sleeping off a drunk, muses: "I just want a lot of it. . . . It's just it itself and you would love them always if they gave it to you. The same one I mean. But they aren't built that way" (244). Where sexual bank accounts are concerned, Marie has more than Dorothy, because Harry has given a lot of it, and only to her, while Dorothy not only gets little from Eddie but even less from her husband who, like most of the wealthy men in this novel, has liver trouble from too much drinking and can't perform any more. Poor Dorothy is left to masturbate her evening away.

Impotence is also the problem of Tommy Bradley, the rich husband of Helene Bradley, who, if consensus means anything, qualifies as the prime bitch of this novel. She too has to have sex, and Tommy, who can't give it, enjoys watching Helene get it, much to the consternation of Richard Gordon, a writer who wilts in the act, thus serving Helene no better than her husband. The local authority on bitches and bitchiness is Dorothy Hollis, who tells us that "bitches have the most fun but you have to be awfully stupid really to be a good one. Like Helene Bradley. Stupid and well-intentioned and really selfish to be a good one" (245). She expects she'll end up as one. In this world—or is it in this Text?—she can find little else to do.

Along with the bitches of this period come the rude writers. The nice rich bitch in "The Snows of Kilimanjaro," who has been a good wife, is resented for having the money that has made Harry's life comfortable. Essentially she exists outside of his life, as he lives his last moments in memories of a past that does not include her. With Harry, who has lived his life, and with that other writer, Richard Gordon, Hemingway seems to be working off, if not out of, his problems with his second wife, Pauline Pfeiffer. And it is to Hemingway's credit here, and throughout his best work, that, in transforming his own quarrels into fiction, he does not give his own surrogates all the best lines. Richard Gordon's wife walks out on him for a nice man (a professor, oddly enough). She tells her husband off in one of the strongest monologues allowed a woman in the Hemingway Text:

> Everything I believed in and everything I cared about I left for you because you were so wonderful and you loved me so much that love was all that mattered. Love was the greatest thing, wasn't it? Love was what we had that no one else had or could ever have? And you were a genius and I was your whole life. I was your partner and your little black flower. Slop. Love is just another dirty lie. Love is ergoapiol pills to make me come around because you were afraid to have a baby. Love is quinine and quinine and quinine until I'm deaf with it. Love is that dirty aborting horror that you took me to. Love is my insides all messed up. It's half catheters and half whirling douches. I know about love. Love always hangs up behind the bathroom door. It smells like lysol. To hell with love. Love is you making me happy and then going off to sleep with your mouth open while I lie awake afraid to say my prayers even because I know I have no right to any more. Love is all the dirty little tricks you taught me that you probably got out of some book. All right. I'm through with you and I'm through with love. Your kind of picknose love. You writer. (185–86)

It is tempting to see in this burst of eloquence Hemingway's rueful acknowledgment of his own failures with women—not as a lover but as a writer. Whether or not this is the case, we must certainly see in this instance how Hemingway can move toward more interesting female characterization by working a transformation of his standard model of bitchery, a transformation that preserves the ego strength of the bitches but justifies their anger or complicates their sexual appetite with other feelings. For Helen Gordon, a thwarted desire for motherhood and a sense of religious guilt energize her language and enrich our sense of her character. In the view of Hemingway's work we are developing here, she belongs with three other women created on a larger scale, all of whom can be usefully seen as transformations of the basic repertory of female figures deployed in Hemingway's earliest work: Lady Brett Ashley of *The Sun Also Rises*, Pilar of *For Whom the Bell Tolls*, and Catherine Bourne of *The Garden of Eden*.

The action of *The Sun Also Rises* opens with Jake Barnes picking up a Paris prostitute, his companion for the evening. This serves as the outer frame for the introduction of Brett; the inner frame is of bitchy dinner conversation and the actual introduction of Brett as the centerpiece in a garland of gay young men. The framing alerts us to read Brett in terms of both a bitchiness and a sexuality that are different from what might be considered normal for women of her position. Not that she is to be seen as representing bitchiness, prostitution, or homosexuality but that she should be seen in relation to these concepts. Like her gypsy proto-type, Carmen, Brett is "unfeminine" in her usurping of the male pre-rogative of promiscuity on her own terms. And the question of whether or not she is a bitch is, in her own view and in that of the text in which she is represented, the central ethical issue of her life. Brett first appears in *The Sun Also Rises* entering a dance club while surrounded by homosexual men, a crowd with whom "one can drink in such safety," as she puts it. Jake Barnes has brought his dinner companion, Georgette, a prostitute he will not touch nor allow to touch him: "You sick?" she asks, and when he says he is, she replies, "Everybody's sick. I'm sick, too" (16). Georgette is swept off to the dance floor by the homosexuals, who are happy to dance with her. Jake, who dislikes them, sees them synechdochically, as fragments of men: "I could see their hands and newly washed, wavy hair in the light from the door. . . . As they went in, under the light I saw white hands, wavy hair, white faces, grimacing, gesturing, talking." Disliking their bodies, Jake disembodies them: "Somehow they made me angry. I know they are supposed to be amusing, and you should be tolerant, but I wanted to swing on one, any one, anything to shatter that superior, simpering composure" (20).

Why such anger? Perhaps because the homosexuals are built like "normal" men yet (Jake might think) do not choose to be "normal," while Jake, who has a "normal" male's sex drive, has been left only fragments of sexual apparatus. He cannot perform, though he desires to do so, while the homosexuals can perform and yet do not desire "normal" heterosexual sex. The sexually fragmented Jake is thus linked to men he perceives in fragments as unmanly because he has himself been unmanned. Indeed, his wound has put him in the passive feminine position of lack and has put Brett in the active position of finding men to provide the apparatus that Jake has lost. Although Brett can maintain a kind of objectivity about her sexual engagements, she suffers from being in love with Jake; while he may find being in love "enjoyable," Brett thinks "it's hell on earth" (27). Yet she must see Jake, and however painful that must be for her, she is willing to pay the price for it. In this novel, the insiders are those who pay their own way and who know the values. While Jake is always careful to pay his own way, as the detailing of his financial transactions makes clear, Brett is frequently being bailed out financially. But her lack of ready cash is beside the point, for Brett has paid in other ways and continues to pay emotionally. After a bout of drinking, Jake muses on this aspect of sexual difference: "I thought I had paid for everything. Not like the woman pays and pays and pays. No idea of retribution or punishment" (148).

In the economy of the text Brett goes on paying even while functioning as a highly valued object of desire. The centrality of her position is
played out at the height of the fiesta—which is, with its bullfights, an
avatar of ancient fertility rites—when Brett is chosen by the garlic-
wreathed riau-riau dancers as "an image to dance around" (155). She
functions here as an unlikely vestal virgin in these ancient rites, and she
succumbs to their power, as exemplified by Pedro Romero, the handsome young bullfighter whom she perceives as the phallus personified.
Irresistibly drawn to him, she enlists Jake's aid in this sexual affair. "I
don't say it's right. It is right though for me. God knows, I've never felt
such a bitch" (184). Romero is drawn to her as well, and he wants to
marry her and make her "more womanly" by having her hair grow out.
She eventually leaves Romero because she knows that she will be bad for
him: "I'm not going to be one of those bitches that ruins children" (243).
She has no religion and not much money, but Brett does have a code of
ethics; having partially recovered from her affair with Romero, she tells
Jake, "You know it makes one feel rather good deciding not to be a
bitch. . . . It's sort of what we have instead of God" (245). As her earlier
statement indicates, Brett has demythologized Romero from the perfect
phallus to the very young man that he is. She thus gives up a lover of
physical and moral perfection for men who are less than perfect but
more her "sort of thing."

In Brett's manner of giving up Romero, Hemingway has allotted her
a moment of maternal feeling that mitigates her masculine image as a
Carmen who loves and leaves whomever she pleases. At the same time,
by presenting her as consciously deciding not to be a bitch, Hemingway
moves her away from that version of female excess—bitchiness—toward a more manly resignation. What makes Brett interesting as a
character is the way that Hemingway has assigned her qualities from
both sides of his gendered repertory of typical figures and situated her

somewhere between the extremes of good and bad behavior on both scales.

If Brett Ashley is a strong woman constructed by complicating and enriching the basic mode of bitchiness, partly by masculinizing that mode, Pilar, in *For Whom the Bell Tolls,* is a strong woman constructed by blending the maternal or nurturing type with that of the manly lesbian on the model of Gertrude Stein. Pilar's strength is a function of her bisexuality. Her character should be read, we are arguing, as one of Hemingway's many explorations of the conundrum of sex and gender, and her own words point us in this direction: "I would have made a good man, but I am all woman and all ugly. Yet many men have loved me and I have loved many men" (*FWBT,* 97). One of the first things we learn about Pilar is that she is ugly and brave—braver than her husband, Pablo, from whom she wrests command of their guerrilla group. Robert Jordan first hears her "deep voice" before he takes her in: "Robert Jordan saw a woman of about fifty almost as big as Pablo, almost as wide as she was tall, in black peasant skirt and waist, with heavy wool socks on heavy legs, black rope-soled shoes and a brown face like a model for a granite monument. She had big but nice looking hands and her curly black hair was twisted into a knot on her neck" (30). In addition, she has "fine grey eyes." Pilar's physical appearance does indeed resemble that of Gertrude Stein as Hemingway described her in *A Moveable Feast:* "Miss Stein was very big but not tall and heavily built like a peasant woman. She had beautiful eyes and a strong German-Jewish face that could also have been Friulano and she reminded me of a northern Italian peasant woman with her clothes, her mobile face and her lovely, thick alive immigrant hair which she wore put up" (14). Both Pilar and Stein are figures of ambiguous gender. Both are perceived as combining a masculine massiveness with feminine qualities. Jo Davidson's marvelous statue of Stein in New York's Bryant Park, though not of granite, illustrates well the monumental quality she shares with Pilar. Both women were seen by Hemingway not only as exemplars of different sexualities but as teachers of these differences. Robert Jordan's ambivalent feelings about Pilar resemble Hemingway's about Stein, to whom he was sexually attracted.

Midway through the novel Robert Jordan puts onions in his morning sandwich, much to the dismay of Agustin, who recoils from the odor. " 'A rose is a rose is an onion,' " responds Jordan. " 'An onion is an onion is an onion' . . . and he thought, a stone is a stein is a rock is a boulder is a pebble" (289). We can read Jordan's language play as Hemingway's little ode of indebtedness to Stein, who taught him not only about language play and speech rhythms but about different modes of sexuality as well (Benstock, 170–73). Just as Hemingway respected Stein's strength as a writer, Jordan respects Pilar's power as a teller of tales—a power so great that he can only hope to write down the stories someday as well as they were told.

Pilar's relationship with Maria, whom she has rescued from a train wreck, is problematical for Robert Jordan and for his creator. The ambivalence Hemingway must have felt about the relationship between Stein and Alice B. Toklas—even though they were godmothers to his first child—is transferred to Pilar in the published text of the novel, but it is even more visible in some of his manuscript revisions, particularly of a scene in which Pilar comes to grips with her feelings about Maria. In this scene Pilar asks Maria to sit and "put thy head in my lap." The manuscript version continues, "Maria moved close to her and laid her head across the woman's big thighs" (K83, 299). In the published version this passage reads, "Maria moved closer to her, put her arms out and folded them as one does who goes to sleep without a pillow and lay with her head on her arms" (154).

When Pilar assures Robert Jordan that he "can have her in a little while," Maria responds, in the published text, "Do not talk like that." After this the manuscript tells us that Maria "stroked her head across the big woman's thighs and patted her hands where they lay" (K83, 299). When Pilar says she is jealous of Maria and Robert Jordan's love affair, Maria protests that Pilar had told her that "there was nothing like that between us." In the manuscript Pilar's reply is, "There is always something like that." She continues: "There is always something that should not be, and for me to find it now in me" (K83, 300). The last nine words are deleted in the published version and replaced with "but with me there is not. Truly there is not," which can be read as a suppression by the author or, more richly, as a repression and excessive protest by Pilar herself. In this interpretation, we may read the manuscript as giving us the very thought that Pilar is repressing in the published text.

As the scene continues in the first draft of the manuscript, Pilar runs her finger "absently, but rememberingly over the line of the girl's cheekbones and over the contours of her cheeks and over her chin and then swept three fingers down the smooth curve of her throat" (K83, 300–301). In the published text this sensuous description, with its paratactic syntax and the iterative clue in "remembering," is abbreviated to "absently but tracingly over the contours of her cheeks." And an additional explicit denial of lesbianism is added: "Listen, *guapa*, I love thee and he can have thee, I am no *tortillera* [lesbian] but a woman made for men." Shortly after this there is another addition in the manuscript margin: "I do not make perversions. I only tell you something true" (K83, 301; novel, 155). And in the final version Pilar's statement to Robert Jordan is entirely suppressed: "There is a darkness in us that you know nothing of. But all have it and I say this to you now" (K83, 300). Whether the novel would have been better with these lines included is not the issue here. Rather, we are reading them as part of the Hemingway Text, and a very revealing part at that. The darkness in women, as we read this Text, is something by virtue of which they are not just mirror images of men who must always desire their opposites (like the bitches in heat of *To Have and Have Not*) but are radically other, contending with men on their own sexual terrain (for more on the revisions to *FWBT* see Gould).

Although the revisions suppress to some extent the eroticism in the relationship between the two women, they do not erase Pilar's bisexuality, which is apparent in her telling Maria that "it gives me pleasure to say thus, in the daytime, that I care for thee" and when she flatly says, "I am jealous" (155). Her bisexuality, and her sense of herself as an erotic force, are visible in her boast to Robert Jordan that when she was young she would have been able to "take the rabbit from thee and thee from the rabbit" (156). As it is, Pilar exercises tremendous power over Maria, a power that angers Jordan but which he does not challenge. Jordan feels that Pilar's power over Maria is not evil, "it was only wanting to keep her hold on life. To keep it through Maria" (176). Spanish women called Pilar usually have the full name of Maria del Pilar. There is a sense, then, that the young Maria represents something of the lost innocence of the older woman, who is also a Maria, and it is Pilar who instructs the innocent beauty in the arts of love.

Pilar is an interesting mixture of the older nurturing female and the erotic wise woman, a creature whose sexuality transcends and threatens any comfortable division of the genders into discrete opposites interested only in one another. In this novel her womanly strength is also defined by Maria's girlish weakness and vulnerability. Maria is defined as beautiful by Pilar, who calls her *guapa* (pretty), and is perceived as the perfect erotic object by Robert Jordan, whose "throat" swells when he looks at her. Robert Jordan and Maria, with her short hair matching his, prefigure the look-alike lovers of *The Garden of Eden*. "You could be brother and sister by the look," Pilar says. "But I believe it is fortunate you are not" (67). To keep the genders straight, however, and to enable

Maria to become the proper object of Robert's love, her hair must be allowed to grow out to shoulder length, "like Garbo in the cinema" (346). Like Catherine in *A Farewell to Arms,* she will play the role of the female figure without troubling subjectivity; Maria is the author's gift to his surrogate, enabling him to experience perfect (and, of course, doomed) love. Maria is one of Hemingway's "girls"—pretty and compliant, part sister and part erotic fantasy—who become interesting as characters only when they bear elements of bitch or whore. But Pilar is a woman and therefore already too complex to blend easily into an erotic fantasy. Her age, her troubling sexuality, and her personal force all seem to require a man constructed on lines comparable to her own. In the Hemingway Text, however, such men are rare and play only minor parts, like Count Mippipopolous in *The Sun Also Rises.* But the girls, and the men who need them, proliferate.

Devils and Daughters "There are, however, no *women* in his books," said Leslie Fiedler in *Love and Death in the American Novel,* going on to note that "he aspires to be not Father but 'Papa,' the Old Man of the girl-child with whom he is temporarily sleeping" (315, 316). This observation is shrewd but not quite accurate (it's hard to be accurate and outrageous at the same time); there are a few *women,* a very few, in the Hemingway Text, but it is true that there are too many girls. *Girl* is a very American term, and the American Girl (along with her mama) became famous when, like James's Daisy Miller and Howells's Florida Vervain, she invaded Europe in search of culture or in hopes of conquering European society with her ingenuous charm and her papa's big bank account. Later the Gibson Girl's looks set a national standard. In the twenties, as women's legs were revealed and the long and supple legs of Josephine Baker enchanted Paris, long-legged American girls became famous in such groups as Busby Berkeley's chorus lines, the Rockettes,

Billy Rose's Long-Stemmed Roses, and so on. In the thirties and forties Petty Girls, Vargas Girls, and pinup girls in general graced magazines (like *Esquire*, where Hemingway's work appeared), calendars, and the lockers of servicemen in World War II. Who of that era can forget the famous pinup of Betty Grable, her curvaceous legs tightly held together, her body a long sinuous line, her coy over-the-shoulder look saying, "I knew you were behind me looking all the time. I felt your gaze." Grable's legs, and those of her poster prototypes, kept up the G.I.'s morale and made the sexually objectified body a patriotic national asset.

American women are frequently called girls even when they are obviously middle-aged women. Those who remember the Vargas and Petty Girls will also remember Helen Hokinson's girls, those bosomy, middle-aged club ladies who populated her *New Yorker* cartoons. To be called a girl, even when you obviously no longer were, was a compliment. The term was intended to allow a woman the pleasant delusion that her youthfulness might be eternal. Its use by Americans signals a refusal to grow up, for the term *woman* carries maternal freight, suggesting a distention and distortion of the female body. Womanhood negates girlhood. Hemingway, who is the mirror of his time in many respects, felt this keenly. It is in this light that we must view the appearance of his wife Pauline in *The Green Hills of Africa* as Poor Old Mama.

Hemingway's fictional girls generally fit an ideal American type: they are long-legged, strong-shouldered, high-cheekboned, slender, and blonde. Even the Spanish girl Maria is given these attributes, and she eagerly looks forward to a Garbo hairdo that will, murmurs Robert Jordan, "hang straight to thy shoulders and curl at the ends as a wave of the sea curls, and it will be the color of ripe wheat" (*FWBT*, 346). He allies Maria to his fantasy women, Garbo and Harlow, who have helped him make it through the night by being "kind and lovely" (137). Maria is a kind of natural fantasy (as opposed to the Hollywood version), compared in her lissomeness to a young tree, a colt, and, for other reasons, to a rabbit. Similarly, Thomas Hudson's movie-star ex-wife (in *Islands in the Stream)* has "silvery ripe-wheat" hair and long lovely legs. As does Dorothy Bridges, and so on.

The girl, as a character type, is usually fatal to Hemingway's writing unless he is able to move the character away from a fantasy of compliant gratification toward womanhood. As Fiedler suggested, this was not an easy task for him, and he found only a few ways of accomplishing it. One was to energize a girl with a dose of bitchiness. A more radical method was to make the character into a "devil." This method is most visible in his later writing, but the possibility was always there in his earlier work and in Judeo-Christian culture itself. Woman has been linked to the devil since the first patriarchal creation myth, in which the devil, in the form of a snake, is the great seducer. And many representations of the "Fall of Man" show the serpent with a woman's torso, thus connecting the feminine and the demonic in cultural memory. In this mode of thought woman becomes the great seductress, the devil's partner if not simply a version of the devil himself. Catherine Bourne is given the name of devil in *The Garden of Eden,* a garden in which she plays the roles of both Eve and Satan. A garden of Eden requires a devil, but we suspect that in this case the devil came first. That Hemingway had women as devils on his mind during the final phase of his work is evident from the slippage of that term into other works, so that Renata (in *Across the River and into the Trees),* Littless (in "The Last Good Country") and Thomas Hudson's first wife (in *Islands in the Stream)* are all called devil at one time or another. In the Hemingway Text girls become devils when they seduce their fall guys into sexual transgressions. And the greatest of these girl-devils is Catherine Bourne.

At the beginning of *The Garden of Eden,* hunger and its satiation exemplify life in the Bournes' earthly paradise. And in this unfallen state indulgence in one pleasure leads inevitably to a desire for the next: the immense hunger for breakfast felt by Catherine in the opening pages of the novel has been caused by intensive early-morning sexual activity. In this economy, one pleasure serves as work to earn the next pleasure. "There was only happiness and loving each other and then hunger and replenishing and starting over" (14). Much of the first chapter, especially in the manuscript version, is given over to chronicling these rituals, which include thorough discussions just after breakfast of what they will have for lunch; that lunch is then lovingly described as well. Lunch is followed by sex; sex is followed by Catherine's trip to the barber for the boy's haircut that signals the beginning of her changes; then aperitifs, then dinner, then a night of sex with breaks for sips of Tavel. This is indeed Hemingway's version of an earthly paradise: a world in which the pleasures of the body are not complicated by the ills of the soul.

The soul and its ills can not be kept at bay for long, however, and it is Catherine who introduces them by interrupting the simple iterative flow of sex and food. She is, as she says, "the destructive type" (5), and her method of destruction is a simple one. Unsatisfied with paradise, she wants "to be changed" (12). The seeds of this desire for change were planted even before the young couple married and entered their earthly paradise. They were planted by a powerful work of art, an image that resonates deeply in this novel: a sculpture by Rodin of a forbidden, transgressive love. In the novel Catherine's desire to change her gender, to alter the sexual dynamic between herself and David, is explicitly traced back to her encounter with this particular work of art. Catherine's boyish haircut is the first outward sign of the statue's effect. When she and David start to make love in the evening to inaugurate this "new" Catherine, she asks him (in the manuscript version) if he remembers "the sculpture in the Rodin museum." He does, and she expects him to know what she wants him to do: to change, "like in the sculpture," which she refers to as *The Metamorphosis* (K422.1/1, 20, 21). Hemingway crossed out this title in the manuscript, presumably preferring to make its identity more mysterious and provocative through David's description: "He knew now and it was like the statue. The one there are no photographs of and of which no reproductions are sold" (K422.1/1, 21). The importance of the sculpture is again asserted at the beginning of Book Two in the manuscript, where Nick and Barbara's story begins and where we are told (with reference to both couples) that "none of them remembered the dates on which they had first turned in off the rue de Varennes to the Hotel Biron with the beautiful gardens and gone into the museum where the changings had started" (K422.1/3).

If the statue's androgynous-looking couple presents a sensuous invitation to sexual exploration when seen as a separate piece, it also presents a warning against such exploration, for the couple, also known as *The Damned Women* (Les Femmes damnées), can be found in the upper right tympanum of Rodin's monumental bronze *Gate of Hell*. The statue carries with it, as we shall see, intertextual references to Ovid, Dante, and Baudelaire, shaped by Rodin's fascination with the erotic. One of the series of titles Rodin gave this work of sculpture was *The Metamorphoses of Ovid* (Les Métamorphoses d'Ovide). The Ovidian text behind the image describes a metamorphosis of gender that carries a warning against homosexual love. In Ovid's story, Iphis, a girl brought up as a boy because her father did not want a female child, falls in love with another girl, Ianthe, but is saved "from abnormality when Iphis is transformed into a man on the eve of her wedding" (Barkan, 70). Iphis herself has perceived her love for Ianthe as a "strange unnatural passion. . . . In all the world of beasts no female ever takes a female" (Ovid, 231). In Ovid's world, as Leonard Barkan points out, "one can earn the right to a transformation that makes one's physical identity accord with the spiritual" (71). Thus Iphis is granted the metamorphosis that validates her "masculine" love for Ianthe.

Another title for the sculpture is *Volupté,* which connects it not to Ovid but to Dante and *The Gate of Hell.* This image would locate the lesbian lovers in Dante's second circle, the place reserved for carnal sinners whose appetites overcame their reason. The very variety of titles Rodin proposed for the work, and the way the image could be transformed by being used in such different contexts as the bronze gates, should help us to understand that Rodin was not trying to represent any particular written text but constructing an image meant to resonate with more than one text. Another of his titles, *Les Fleurs du mal* (Flowers of evil), connects the sculpture to Baudelaire's series of poems with that collective title. The sculpture is in fact one of a group of images of entwined androgynous and female bodies, the models for which were two lesbian dancers from the Paris Opera. John Tancock has pointed out that "Rodin liked to give his works any number of titles, inspired by the forms he created rather than inspiring the finished work," and he sees in the interchangeability of the titles an equivalence with Rodin's interest in sexual fluidity or metamorphosis (Tancock, 259–60). The *Metamorphoses* entered the collections of the Musée Rodin between 1927 and 1931. In May 1927 Hemingway and his second wife, Pauline, honeymooned at Le Grau-du-Roi and then returned to Paris, where they had an apartment. The Hemingways were in Paris at various times between 1927 and 1931, so it is not unlikely that they visited the Rodin museum and noticed the sculpture. And in 1948 Ernest gave his fourth wife, Mary, a copy of Baudelaire's *Les Fleurs du mal* in a limited edition, illustrated by Rodin. The illustration for poem LXXXI, "Femmes damnées," is of two seated nude women embracing in a pose reminiscent of the couple in bronze.

In *The Garden of Eden,* David and Catherine Bourne quickly begin speaking of their new sexual adventures in a language drawn from cultural and religious discourses that regard such activities as abhorrent. They do this, perhaps, because the language of condemnation adds a further thrill to the enterprise, but it is not easy to say how deeply they share or how fully they might reject this discourse. Nor is it easy to locate Hemingway himself on the matter. But let us look at the language itself. When Catherine plays a feminine role she calls herself a good girl. When she switches to a masculine role, she is called, in David's terminology, Devil. David worries about what will become of them: "What can there be that will not burn out in a fire that rages like that." Fires of lust, fires of hell. It is David who connects them through the statue and its references, addressing himself, "You know the statue moved you and why shouldn't it?" (K422.1/1, 23). He feels guilty about having been moved by the statue but denies that he should feel that way, asking "why" it shouldn't have moved him.

Hemingway's interest in lesbianism and female bisexuality, which was exceptional for a man of his time and type, is a topic we shall investigate more deeply in Chapter 3, but we must pause to consider it here because of the way it intersects with his development of female characters. We assume that many readers would agree with us that Brett, Pilar, and Catherine Bourne are three of Hemingway's most compelling female characters—perhaps the strongest characterizations of women to be found in his longer works. That is, they are strong characters and, despite their weaknesses, strong women. We now suggest that the strength of these fictional figures can be understood in terms of the way that Hemingway has transformed his stock repertory of bitch, Mummy, and girl. Brett is a bitch who renounces bitchery. She is also a woman who behaves with a sexual aggressiveness often assumed to be a male prerogative. Pilar is a maternal figure with a past of sexual—and even bisexual—aggressiveness that she has put aside, either because of her age or, as Hemingway's men do, to get on with the war, in which she has assumed a male role. And Catherine Bourne is a girl who transcends submissive girlhood through her desire for a metamorphosis of gender that will enable her to play a male role both in bed and in her aggressive pursuit of Marita, who enters the text as an interesting lesbian only to metamorphose into a submissive daughter-lover, like Renata of *Across the River and into the Trees*.

William Butler Yeats once wrote that he made rhetoric out of his quarrels with others and poetry out of his quarrels with himself. Ernest Hemingway, it seems to us, made feeble female characters out of his dreams of erotic wish fulfillment and strong ones out of his nightmares. His interest in women who appropriated "male" qualities or prerogatives was stimulated, no doubt, by women he encountered regularly in his Paris days, but it was also a function of his French reading. If the *Carmen* of Merimée can be detected behind *The Sun Also Rises*, Gautier's *Mademoiselle de Maupin* lurks around *The Garden of Eden*. Gautier's youthful novel (1835) is remembered now mainly for its preface, with its scathing attack on bourgeois critics and readers, but Hemingway, who may have enjoyed the attack on critics, seems to have been interested in the story itself. He had a copy of the novel in Key West (Reynolds 1981, 129), and he included it on the list of current reading by Thomas Hudson's young son Tom in *Islands in the Stream*. Tom mentions these books in the context of his reading of Joyce's *Ulysses*, which nearly got him expelled from boarding school for having "a dirty mind" (*IS*, 68). In the manuscript for *The Garden of Eden*, Marita and David mention *Mademoiselle de Maupin* in their discussion of erotic literature and transvestism. (They also mention Gogol's *Taras Bulba*.) David describes *Mademoiselle de Maupin* as "what we do made into musical comedy," and he asks Marita if it gave her "an erection" when she read it. "Of course," she replies, "Didn't it you?" "Sure," says David. "That's why he wrote it. For himself and for his friends. That's how all books that are just fun are written" (K422.1/36, 22).

Gautier's Madelaine de Maupin is a young woman who disguises herself as a man to learn what was behind the "conventional masks" men wore when in the presence of women (Gautier, 149). "She wished to be acquainted with men before giving herself to a man" (158). As a result of her cross-dressing she begins to lose her sexual identity: "In truth, neither of the two sexes are mine; I have not the imbecile submission, the timidity or the littleness of women; I have not the vices, the disgusting intemperance, or the brutal propensities of men: I belong to a third, distinct sex, which as yet has no name" (177). The adventures of this person of nameless sexuality end with a night in which she makes love to partners of both sexes. Gautier's treatment of the subject is humorous, and he allows his bisexual heroine, Madelaine-Théodore, to ride off and leave her lovers forever, telling one of them, D'Albert, in a letter, "For the beauty that I gave you, you repaid me with pleasure; we are quits" (292). Thus passion is reduced to a simple fair exchange, and Madelaine escapes unscathed and with the knowledge she sought. Hemingway often dreamed of just such a reduction of emotional matters to a simple system of exchange (Comley 1979), but in both life and art he never managed to take love lightly. And when it came to sexual transgressions he was more like Baudelaire and Rodin, who could not contemplate such matters without a cloud of hellfire hovering over them, making such transgressions both more interesting and more dangerous.

Gautier discreetly avoided recounting Madelaine's experience of making love to Rosette (who believes Madelaine is Théodore), closing the door on their amours and allowing the reader the "liberty to draw thence any references that he likes" (290). What it was like for Madelaine to actually be Théodore is not something about which he seems very concerned. Nor does he suggest that the business of crossing sexual boundaries might cause the adventurer any psychic distress. Neither Madelaine pretending to be Théodore nor Gautier pretending to be Madelaine is a serious matter for the author. For Rodin, however, the representation of the female body constituted an attempt at imaginative metamorphosis for the artist himself. Catherine Lampert has described Rodin's motive as a desire to "inhabit his subject. . . . What the aging Rodin is desperate to discover but cannot, as he realizes, is to 'know' what it is like from the other side. What sensations female languor, lust, lesbian pleasing, manual stimulation and finally ecstasy are comprised of" (171). Though he knew Gautier's book, Hemingway's approach to sexual metamorphosis is more like Rodin's than Gautier's. That is, his characters are fascinated by sexual metamorphoses because he is so fascinated himself—as a man and as a writer who could use this issue, which he called "sea change," in constructing characters and situations.

For Catherine Bourne, to experience what boys feel is to transgress, to break a taboo that is not merely social but religious. Such transgression, linked as it is to darkness and damnation, is coded in the Hemingway Text as madness. After such knowledge, as T. S. Eliot would put it, what forgiveness? Nick and Barbara, who engage in such transgression in the manuscript of *The Garden of Eden*, are also cursed: he is killed in an accident while she is being unfaithful to him, and she, burdened with guilt and grief, commits suicide in Venice. In Hemingway's garden the women follow Eve's pattern, seeking forbidden knowledge, and the men follow the women more cautiously, seeking new sensations, though they are a little leery of them. Though David tries to reassure himself, "a sin is what you feel bad after and you don't feel bad" (K422.1/1, 24), the text informs us that his last transgression with Catherine "hurt him all the way through." Physically? Emotionally? Hemingway will not say, nor will he provide readers graphic descriptions of the logistics of these sexual changings, leaving one befuddled critic to suggest that "somehow, she sodomizes him." David is presented as aroused by the Rodin sculpture but damaged by an attempt to capture in life the stylized passion of that art.

The line between life and art is one crucial division in the world of *The Garden of Eden*. The line between the bedroom and the rest of life parallels the first. Catherine seeks to extend her change from the private world of erotic bliss into the public world of museums and restaurants. She, like Madelaine de Maupin, wants to experience being male as completely as she can. But David Bourne, like all those male characters in the Hemingway Text who resemble Ernest himself, is incapable of imaginatively assuming a female position—except for those private erotic moments that leave him stricken with remorse. He knows that these transgressions have made him a better writer, but he feels that he has "deteriorated morally" in paying for this improvement (K422.1/17, 9bis).

It is hard to say just how deeply either David or Ernest believe in this priggish terminology. We are inclined to read it as masking another sort of resistance: a reluctance to assume a female position in life, which is one of the sustaining forces behind homophobia. This reluctance is grounded in the fear of castration implied by assuming a feminine role. To wish to be a woman, as Karen Horney pointed out long ago, is to wish for castration (see Courtivron, 223–24). In *The Garden of Eden*, then, Hemingway has positioned his surrogate, David Bourne, in an intolerable double bind: the source of his creativity lies in what for him is the forbidden territory of the feminine. Hemingway's mentor, Sherwood Anderson, had provided him with an example of the horror associated with this territory in "The Man Who Became a Woman." One of Anderson's young men who hang around horses—men who would rather rub their hands over them than over human bodies—one night looks at himself in the mirror behind a bar and sees "a girl's face, and a lonesome and scared girl too" (Anderson, 207). Later, sleeping in the loft above the stable of his favorite horse, he is found by "two big buck niggers" who are drunk and, seeing his body—"pretty white and slender then, like a young girl's body"—take him for a girl. He escapes, feeling that he has become the "kind of princess" he has dreamed about. In a nightmare chase he stumbles through a landscape fraught with the imagined terror of rape and of death, which takes the form of a field of horse's bones. Anderson being Anderson, the boy discovers finally that he is "a man and my own self," whatever that may mean. The story is a psychoanalyst's delight—a blatant example of male fears about becoming female in a text Hemingway must have known. In particular, Anderson's use of the mirror in this story prefigures Hemingway's in some of the works we shall be discussing in the next chapter.

Catherine Bourne has no similar fear, for she has everything to gain in becoming a boy. As a boy, she can "do anything and anything and anything" (*GofE*, 15) or, to put it in the clinical terms of Karen Horney, "The identification with the father is confirmed by old wishes tending in the same direction and it does not carry with it any sort of feeling of guilt but rather a sense of acquittal" (Courtivron, 224). For Catherine, assuming the role of a boy is not simply an erotic thrill but a social enablement. She has found being a girl a "god damned bore," and she associates femininity with "scenes, hysteria, false accusations, temperament" (*GofE*, 70). We must assume that Hemingway made these associations as well and that Catherine's attempt to transcend girlhood constitutes Hemingway's attempt to transcend his own limits as a writer. The danger for him as a constructor of character was that his males might be too much like himself and his females as insipid as those of a boyish daydream. One solution that he found—possibly the most important one—was to make his women more like himself and to make his men, as we shall see, more feminine. In the case of Catherine, however, there are limits to how far Hemingway could bring her into what he saw as a world of masculine creative potency.

Like other Hemingway bitches—but unlike his girls—Catherine is eloquent. But no woman in the Hemingway Text is a serious writer. When Catherine's desire to experience maleness leads her to writing she reaches a boundary neither she nor Hemingway can cross. David is the writer in this family, just as Nick is the real painter and Barbara a pale imitation in the other couple who once inhabited this *Garden of Eden*. And David becomes a better writer as he is led into femininity by his devil. But this territory of creative textuality cannot be reached by a woman who seeks to appropriate masculinity. The experiences that lead David to heightened powers lead Catherine to madness. Hemingway has done all he can to make Catherine an interesting figure, giving her attributes drawn from his wives, from Zelda Fitzgerald, and even from his mother—but he cannot allow her into his own preserve of masculinity. David writes. Catherine cheers him on when he writes about the two of them—that is, when she enters his textual world and can see herself reflected there. But she hates the cruelty and bestiality of his African stories and is jealous of his attempts to give his father textual life. She believes that her money has enabled David to work, and it is certainly the case, whether she is conscious of it or not, that her sexual creativity has stimulated his African writing as well as his writing of the narrative of their life together. In her mind these two texts are rivals, and she has proprietary rights over both of them. She demonstrates these rights by an act of destruction, burning David's African manuscript in the yard of the hotel as Nick Adams' mother burned the doctor's Indian artifacts in the yard of their house. Her thwarted creativity—thwarted because, in the Hemingway Text, this is a boundary no woman can cross—turns her into the puritanical castrating mother who destroys her boy-man's connection to the primitive. Because she is also the devil of this Eden, transgressing the divine edict regarding sexual boundaries, she has become an impossible figure for which the Hemingway Text has no role except madwoman. Seeing her as mad enables both David and Hemingway, the God of this Eden, to maintain their sympathy for her. Hemingway's sympathy is manifested especially by his allowing Catherine to be both mad and sane, with one quality uppermost at any given time while the other remains visible. In her final letter, the last words we hear from her in the published text, she is superbly sane and self-aware, but it is still the letter of a smart and troubled person rather than that of a "writer."

Hemingway's struggle to construct a novel called *The Garden of Eden* is one of the most revealing sections of the entire Hemingway Text, though the marketers of the unfinished product have tried to erase the signs of this struggle wherever possible. When he began writing this book, Hemingway had two characters named Catherine (or two versions of one character), both of whom were mentally unstable. One Catherine became Barbara during revisions. Both women are obsessively interested in hair, their husbands' as well as their own, and with being "just the same" as their husbands in physical appearance. Both characters want narratives written about their married lives. Barbara, who is a bit older than Catherine, is unable to have a baby. Catherine thinks she, too, is sterile. Like her husband, Nick Sheldon, Barbara is a painter, but she no longer paints. "I painted well enough for a woman. But not well enough to interest me," she says, adding, "How can I paint with Nick painting the way he does? Nick's all I care about" (K422.5/4, 16). Another character dropped from the published version of the book, a writer named Andy, suggests that Barbara stopped painting because it was too revelatory: "Her painting worried me and I think it worried her too. It was very close to the edge and that shows clearer in painting than in anything else" (K422.7, 26). Both women have initiated sexual changing under the influence of the Rodin bronze. Although Barbara is not referred to as a devil, she thinks of herself in that way. Speaking of her inability to have a baby, she says to Nick, "Well at least I haven't devilled you about things like that any more" (K422.7, 33).

Barbara is strongly attracted to Catherine—so much so that she begs David to "get her out of here" because Catherine is destructive and "I'm destroy material" (K422.5/4, 12, 14–15). She finds Catherine's features especially attractive, telling David, "You know no man ever looked at her that didn't have an erection. I don't know what women have but whatever it is I have it" (K422.5/4, 12). Yet she hastens to add, "I know I'm strange. But I'm not a queer or I never was." It is something special about Catherine, apparently, that causes those around her to break sexual taboos. But Barbara is also in some sense a version of Catherine. That is, as Hemingway worked on the manuscript, he deployed two versions of the same character rather than simply replacing one with the other. Like Catherine, Barbara is obsessed with gender transformation, but she seems more aware of the dangers involved, acknowledging that she is "crazy if you like and with special things or one thing that I wanted and got it or have it or had it. It was just a simple delight or ecstacy [sic]. It was private but I made it public. That's the danger. The necessary danger. And I didn't know things took possession of you. That's when you've gone wrong of course" (K422.5/4, 14). What is wrong, of course, is that when a wife goes public with her boyishness in the Hemingway Text it feminizes her husband—in public. And being feminized was something that both Hemingway and his male characters brooded about and feared.

Barbara's obsessiveness is demonstrated in the first chapter of Book Two of the manuscript. She lies awake and muses à la Molly Bloom about hair and the "wicked" thing she has done in getting Nick to grow his hair long. The whole first chapter concerns hair, and their discussions of it excite Nick and Barbara so much that they regularly fall into bed and make love while discussing it. Meanwhile, the Bournes are busy trimming and bleaching their respective heads of hair and feeling just as wicked as Nick and Barbara. These shenanigans have led Mark Spilka to refer to the book as Hemingway's "Barber Shop Quartet," an almost irresistible gibe for those who do not see the importance of being earnest about hair. But hair, in the Hemingway Text, functions as a visible sign of sexual transgression, a public challenge to public notions of sexual propriety that are both fragile and dangerously powerful—especially for those who have internalized them to the point of self-demonization for transgressions.

Perhaps sensing that hairstyles could not carry all the weight he was putting on them, Hemingway wrote a script for Barbara that caused her to violate a sexual taboo more seriously inscribed in public morality. Though there is no shortage of erotic activity at home, Barbara nevertheless initiates an affair with Andy while continuing to insist on her love for Nick. This move connects her to the insatiable bitches of Hemingway's earlier work, and it provides the occasion for the punishment of her transgressions. When Barbara discovers that Nick has been killed in an accident at the very time she and Andy were making love, she is overwhelmed with a remorse that ends only with her suicide while in Venice with Andy, who (we beg the reader to indulge our lapse into soap opera syntax as we try to follow these tangles) throughout all this has found his writing improving, just as David's improves with his corruption under Catherine's tutelage. There is a touch of Baudelaire in Hemingway's assumption of the writer's need for corruption—and of Joyce as well.

Two madwomen, as it turned out, were more than Hemingway could handle, especially when paired with the difficulty of writing the lives of three male artists along with the complexity of doubling plots and characters. But why did the women have to be mad? And why were they denied a level of creativity comparable to that attained by the men? Those who find comfort in assigning biographical causes for aesthetic effects will find ample material in Hemingway's difficulties with such women writers as Gertrude Stein and his third wife, Martha Gellhorn, and in his view of his mother's relationship with his father and Zelda Fitzgerald's with Scott. But he also inherited a massive load of cultural baggage, which he shared with other male modernists, to the effect that women lacked something essential to genius. (This view was carried to the point of caricature by Otto Weininger in *Sex and Character,* a book that was important to modernists ranging from Gertrude Stein to Wittgenstein.) From where Hemingway was positioned, the best he had to offer was madness, and the best madness he could fashion was what he finally gave to Catherine Bourne, complete with a logic that could make the irrational sound as rational as you please and with the further capacity to turn reason on her own madness and discuss it.

Of all Hemingway's girls, Catherine Bourne is by far the most interesting (just as Brett Ashley is the most interesting of his bitches). Hemingway may have made her mad, but he also made her smart and witty, and in this novel it is mainly her mad wit that moves the narrative along and prevents what she and David are doing from descending into a bog of steamy forbidden sex. Catherine is far more interesting than Marita, the lesbian sex-kitten she brings home for her and David to play with and who turns out to be dangerous precisely because she keeps her claws sheathed most of the time. Marita's willingness to accommodate both Bournes sexually and her occasional sharpness of tongue with Catherine suggest that her lineage is that of Hemingway's other bitches, but, in the published book, she metamorphoses into a sister-lover, a girl who is all adoration and encouragement for her genius of a man. In the manuscript, as we shall see in the next chapter, things are more complicated, but what is obvious even in the published novel is that the figure of the too-perfect, too-submissive girl is a seductive poison for Hemingway as a creator of female characters, encouraging him to write as Freud said children dream: of the direct fulfillment of wishes rather than through the displacements and inversions of the mature dreamwork.

These figures of girl and devil haunt the other late fiction of Hemingway, both the works published while he was alive and those edited and published after his death. In *Islands in the Stream*, for instance, Thomas Hudson, a painter like Nick Sheldon of *The Garden of Eden* manuscript, divests himself of family and women to go and meet his death hunting submarines. His last female visitor is his first wife, a movie star whom he still loves and who is currently entertaining the troops. She is greeted as devil, and after a spot of sex for old time's sake she is bid adieu as devil again. Her final appearance in the book occurs when Hudson is at sea, sleeping with his .357 magnum between his legs, when in a dream she comes to lie on top of him and asks, "Should I be you or you be me?" She coaches him in this sexual transformation by telling him to "lose everything," swinging her silky hair across his face. "Will you give up everything? Are you glad that I brought back the boys and that I come and be a devil in the night?" (*IS*, 44). This is another version of Catherine Bourne (or perhaps Marita), but it is now operating explicitly on the level of dream itself, reminding us of how dangerously close to dream many of the late Hemingway fictions actually are.

With his devil present only in dreams, Hudson lives in a wet world of guns and men, from which he can take his leave in a manly way, as Colonel Cantwell does in *Across the River and into the Trees*, free of emotional clutter and female seduction. For Cantwell belongs to this same segment of the Hemingway Text, in which the unfinished *Garden of Eden* (begun in 1946 and worked on at intervals thereafter) regularly makes itself felt. In the Venice of *Across the River* Cantwell acts out an older man's fantasy of a perfect, incestuous love. To the teen-age Renata he says, "I love you, devil. And you're my Daughter, too" (114). Renata is endowed by her creator with a "wonderful, long, young, lithe and properly built body" (109), and she loves the colonel (her Papa figure because she seems to have no other) unreservedly and adoringly. Since she is his "last" true love, she must be perfect, and so she is: unspoiled, virginal, a caricature of compliance, a pretty ear for an old soldier's reminiscences of war. Like Catherine Bourne, she wants to be like her lover: "I want to be like you. Can I be like you a little while tonight?" (142). But when she tries to give him a gentle order ("You are going to have to tell [more war stories] to me later"), he stares at her brutally and says, *"Have to?"* Tears come to her eyes and she pitifully says, "But I don't wish to command. . . . I wish to serve you" (143). Clearly we are back in Catherine Barkley country again.

Of the portrait of herself that Renata will give the Colonel, he says he will say when asked that it is a portrait of his daughter, for he, like his maker, has always wanted a daughter. "I can be your daughter as well as everything else," she says. When he suggests "that would be incest," she brushes the thought aside, saying that incest would not be so terrible in Venice, given its history. (Including literary history. The elderly Aschenbach's fascination with a beautiful boy in *Death in Venice* provides a sinister backdrop to this old man's fascination with a girl.) Exactly what does go on, sexually speaking, is too coyly presented to raise anyone's Beatrice Cenci antennae. Shortly after their incest exchange, Renata tells the colonel, "I have a disappointment for you," which, for the colonel, is like hearing that he has lost a battalion to the enemy. Bravely, he responds, "My poor Daughter," thinking, "Now there was nothing dark about the word and she was his Daughter, truly, and he pitied her and loved her" (110). The disappointment, we must assume, is that she has her period, since earlier, given a choice of constellations, she has chosen to be the moon (99). In a manuscript draft of this text she was a little more specific about the "disappointment." " 'And the famous hay,' she said. 'You remember the famous hay that was in the Noel Coward play? I cannot go to the famous hay now' " (K1/4, 170). Coward's play, *Hay Fever,* is about people jumping into bed with one another. In place of hitting the hay, Renata is willing to be kissed and to hold or be stroked by the colonel's scarred and, to him, ugly hand. This "bad hand," as the colonel calls it, is very active when the two are messing about in a gondola. The hand, "which had been shot through twice," is much admired by Renata, who dreams about it: "a strange mixed-up dream and I dreamed it was the hand of our Lord" (84). The apotheosis of Colonel Cantwell (or at least his hand) can scarcely be seen as anything but embarrassing, even if we take "our Lord" to refer not to God himself but to Ernest Hemingway, who is the Papa of this little universe. In the course of the novel, the colonel also thinks of himself in relation to the tragic heroes Lear (171), who loved one daughter very much but lost her, and Othello (240), an old soldier from another country who loved a Venetian girl "not wisely but too well," causing her death before taking his own. But *Across the River and into the Trees* is an *Othello* without an Iago, a *Tempest* without the disruptive strangers who initiate the plot, an Eden from which even the pseudo-devil of a pretended incest is banished, a *Death in Venice* without the plague.

It is as if, throughout his later work, Hemingway sensed the need for some demonic presence, a counterforce to wish-fulfillment that could energize a plot. His struggles with the girl-devil combination are a symptom of this need and his awareness of it. In a late Nick Adams story, the unfinished "Last Good Country," we find him trying again to work this combination in the character of Littless. She is teen-aged Nick's little sister, reminiscent of Helen, Krebs's "favorite sister" in "Soldier's Home," who pitches better than the boys and who considers her brother her beau. Littless accompanies Nick into the woods on an endless (because unfinished) adventure of escape from adult rules. This story is more fantastic than the other Nick Adams stories, and in it the intimacy of Nick and his sister seems to threaten the incest taboo. Their escape to the woods is also an escape from society's rules about sexual behavior and gender status. Littless wants to be a boy, so she hacks off her hair, hoping to pass for one. She says to Nick, in language that evokes the specter of Catherine Bourne, "Now I'm your sister but I'm a boy too. Do you think it will change me into a boy?" (*CSS*, 531). Nick says no and tells her, "I don't want to trade you for a brother." Littless, "tanned brown" and with dark brown eyes and dark brown hair, resembles Hemingway's sister Carol, the one who looked most like him, and also Nick's Indian lover, Trudy. As for these fictional siblings, "she and Nick loved each other and they did not love the others" (504).

How did they love each other? Watching her sleep, Nick notices her high cheekbones and long lashes. "He loved his sister very much and she loved him too much. But, he thought, I guess these things straighten out" (535). But when she awakens in the morning and asks him if she slept too late, he replies, "No, devil" (536), which, as we have seen, is an equivocal term of endearment used by adult males for their lovers, and most specifically for lovers like Catherine Bourne, who transgress society's approved sexual boundaries. The slippage of such terminology across the Hemingway Text suggests a loss of authorial control over this brother-sister relationship that may have made it difficult for Hemingway to complete this as a Nick Adams story. Philip Young, who edited the story for his edition of *The Nick Adams Stories*, may have been worried about this too, for he tried to clean it up a bit, leaving out a chunk of dialogue about Trudy and the fact that Nick has impregnated her at least once. Also missing is a bit of dialogue in which Littless differentiates between the wrong they are doing and "that kind of wrong like you and Trudy [did]" (K542/1, 3). Another manuscript fragment has Littless asking, "It isn't dirty for a brother and sister to love each other is it?" She asks because "somebody in the family" said it was (K545, 4 i-j).

In this last return to a time and place of remembered happiness, Hemingway presents the teenage Nick with a smaller, younger, female mirror of himself, a nonthreatening good companion trained by her beloved brother to be a good camper. Together, these feminine and masculine projections of himself could repeat those comforting rituals of camping and fishing that had renewed Nick's war-damaged self in the early and much-acclaimed "Big Two-Hearted River." In that story there was no feminine element present, the feminine being one of those complications best avoided—like the swamp—by a man in Nick's delicate psychic condition. In Hemingway's later writing, we are suggesting, the swamp is replaced by the notion of a Garden of Eden, too alluring to be avoided but possibly swampy in its essence. In the wilderness Eden of "The Last Good Country," Littless plays Catherine Bourne's role of thief-girl ("I like to be thief girl" [K422.5/5, 10]), reminding Nick (in the manuscript) that "I've stolen for you and I keep your secrets" (K542/1, 3).

Littless' dark rival in this story is Trudy the Ojibway, a Marita of the woods who has borne Nick's child and thus fulfilled his mother's worst fears about primitivism. The fantasy of a darker woman, possessed of a sexual knowledge that good little white girls do not have, is a thread running through Hemingway's later writing—and indeed, his life—that we will unravel more completely in the next chapter. For the moment, however, it will suffice to note that Nick is described in this story as thinking, "You should have been an Indian. . . . It would have saved you a lot of trouble" (CSS, 530). Indian or not, in this story Nick wants to see Trudy again for a "kiss" before he goes away from the last good country. This bothers Littless, though she finally admits that she knows where Trudy can be found. When Nick asks why she didn't tell him earlier, Littless (in a section omitted from the published version) tries her own brand of seduction. "Nicky you ought to learn not to ask too much. I thought we'd go away together and I'd take care of you and you'd take care of me and you know where I thought we'd go. I thought we'd hunt and fish and eat and read and sleep together and not worry and love each other and be kind and good" (K 542/1, 12). As they start their journey and Littless promises not to talk about Trudy any more, Nick says, "The hell with Trudy" (514). Sometimes the white magic of incest is stronger than the black magic of miscegenation.

This uncompleted story ends as Nick prepares to read *Wuthering Heights* to Littless. Earlier he had said that two of the books his sister had chosen to bring along on their flight from civilization were "too old" for her. Now, when Littless asks, "Is it too old to read out loud to me?" Nick answers no, suggesting that Littless is now ready to hear the story of Heathcliff and Catherine, whose oneness is similar to theirs and whose union would have been akin to incest. "The Last Good Country" has no end because Hemingway could not write it. This problem was so acute for him that it actually entered the text he was trying to write. In the final bit of (manuscript) dialogue after Nick has picked up *Wuthering Heights* to read, Littless asks, "Why don't you write anymore?" and Nick (or Ernest) answers, "I can't write and worry and be in trouble all the time" (K542/2, 102—page crossed out). This section was crossed out in the manuscript, which Hemingway left unfinished in July 1958. Where could this story have gone? Toward the swampy Garden of Eden, with Nick and his boyish sister committing homoerotic incest? The alternative would be to go back to Mummy, ("our Mother," as Littless calls her), which would be to admit that there was no "good country" to escape to any more, and that all such attempts ended in the suffocating enclosure of the darkened bedroom where Mummy lies.

3 Sea Changes and Tribal Things

You have no precedent to help you and you write about a country where no one has written truly to guide you. They've written well about South Africa but not about the highlands on the equator where you were a boy. They will of course but so far it is yours to do as well with it as you can. You must do it better than anyone ever can and never leave out anything because you are ashamed of it or because no one would ever understand. You must not let the ["white taboos"—crossed out in manuscript] things you must not say nor write because you are white and will go back there affect you at all and you must not deny or forget all the tribal things that are as important. The tribal things are more important really.
—*The Garden of Eden,* manuscript (K422.1/23)

The quotation above is from a section of manuscript omitted from the published version of *The Garden of Eden* (K422.1/23, 9–10). This passage might seem to suggest that tribal things refer only an insider's knowledge, the sort of "true" knowledge of Africa that a white visitor could never come to attain. In this chapter, however, we argue that tribal things also have an erotic significance developed explicitly in the manuscript of *The Garden of Eden* but foreshadowed in many parts of the larger Hemingway Text. In taking the metaphor of text as texture literally, we trace several threads that over the years became woven into a pattern of associations, a figure in the Hemingway carpet. These threads or themes are the search for truth itself and the means to express it; an interest in races and peoples seen as "darker" and more "primitive" than Euro-Americans; and a fascination (attraction and repulsion) with transgressive sexuality. Hemingway's continuing interest as a writer, it seems to us, is due not merely to the stylistic gloss of his best writing but also to the way he combined these themes and made them his own. In the previous chapter we showed how some of Hemingway's strongest characterizations grew from a repertory of simple types. Here we show how interesting thematic complexities emerge from the intersection of a few basic preoccupations or concerns.

Let us begin with the thread of truth. Most writers of fiction since

Cervantes have been obsessed with finding the truth behind the deceptive appearances of the world. Hemingway was no exception, and his journalistic training only confirmed and formalized his perpetual search for the accurate information he called the true gen. Once upon a time Sigmund Freud worried about children whose curiosity concerning sexual matters was frustrated by the lies and evasions of their parents. In "The Sexual Enlightenment of Children" Freud wrote that all desire for learning was grounded on every child's first great quest for truth—the truth about sex. If this first quest were frustrated, Freud wrote, the child's desire to learn about things in general might be impaired. The Hemingway Text confirms and modifies Freud's point. Nick Adams' father, like most parents of his day, was "unsound on sex." How unsound emerges in these lines from "Fathers and Sons":

> One morning he read in the paper that Enrico Caruso had been arrested for mashing.
>
> "What is mashing?"
>
> "It is one of the most heinous of crimes," his father answered. Nick's imagination pictured the great tenor doing something strange, bizarre, and heinous with a potato masher to a beautiful lady who looked like the pictures of Anna Held on the inside of cigar boxes. He resolved, with considerable horror, that when he was old enough he would try mashing at least once.
>
> His father had summed up the whole matter by stating that masturbation produced blindness, insanity, and death, while a man who went with prostitutes would contract hideous venereal diseases and that the thing to do was to keep your hands off of people. (*CSS*, 259)

Young Ernest's reaction to this kind of misinformation was not the repression of all intellectual curiosity that Freud feared might result. He apparently learned early what he wrote down many years later: "You could believe nothing your parents told you after a certain age because you had the example of their lives before you and you knew that whatever happened to your own life it should not be like that" (K383, 6). Nevertheless, it seems apparent in Hemingway's work, and especially in the manuscripts and posthumously published materials that are now becoming available, that he did not emerge unscathed from his early quest for the truth on human sexuality.

We are not interested in reducing Hemingway to some Oedipal formula that would obscure the unique features of his own way of organizing sexual materials in his life and work. But the life and work themselves—the Hemingway Text—present us with certain patterns that are too insistent to ignore. One of these patterns concerns a relation between the truths of sexuality and truth in general, which are linked in the Hemingway Text. As we have come to understand it, the bond between sexuality and truth for Hemingway was a matter of the primitive or primal. The link between sex and truth was based on their common opposition to the lies and deceits of culture as embodied, for instance, in the lies told by Nick's and Ernest's fathers to their sons. Every attentive reader of his work knows that Hemingway took a special interest in situations in which truth emerges because life is on the line and death is near in war or blood sport. But even attentive readers have been reluctant to follow the more complicated patterning of sexuality and truth in the Hemingway Text. One reason for this diffidence may be that sexual truths, for Hemingway, lie not at the center of "standard" heterosexual practice—as they do so notoriously for D. H. Lawrence—but at the margins: in what the society of Hemingway's parents would have called perversion or miscegenation. These motifs— sex across racial boundaries and sex that violates cultural taboos—are the warp and woof of sexuality in the Hemingway Text. We shall explore the pattern they make.

We begin our discussion of this pattern by putting together two of Hemingway's strangest analogies, drawn from two of his strangest stories:

> They found Touraine to be a very flat hot country very much like Kansas. ("Mr. and Mrs. Elliot"; *CSS,* 125)

> In those days the distances were all very different, the dirt blew off the hills that have now been cut down, and Kansas City was very like Constantinople. ("God Rest You Merry, Gentlemen"; *CSS,* 198)

One of the oddities that link these sentences is that the word *very* appears twice in each of them. One could write a whole essay on Hemingway's verys, but let us say only that our consideration of his use of the word in a number of texts has led us to believe that he often uses it satirically, as in "A Very Short Story" (Scholes, 110) and that it is frequently an index of his personal investment in the events and characters presented in the text. In this case, however, the important components of these two sentences lie elsewhere. Each sentence emphasizes a simile, and both similes are very strange indeed: the Château country of the Loire valley (Touraine) and the city that was once Byzantium (Constantinople, now Istanbul) are compared with the state of Kansas and with Kansas City. What strikes one first is the inappropriateness, the farfetchedness of the comparisons. Two of the most exotic and storied places in the world are connected with a name that has become legendary for lack of interest, at least since *The Wizard of Oz.* (And please do not tell us that Kansas City is actually in Missouri and is a very interesting place. It is still a long way, in every sense of the expression, from Constantinople.) If we can agree that Kansas and Kansas City represent something similar in these comparisons—something quintessentially American, something provincial, something historically insignificant—and that Touraine and Constantinople represent the exotic, the cultured, the significant, then we can perhaps agree also that the point of these similes must lie in their very strangeness, in what we might call their perversity.

The comparison with Constantinople, which is in fact the opening sentence of "God Rest You Merry, Gentlemen," is presented in the form of a negation. Kansas City was like Constantinople before it was mutilated by having its hills "cut down." "You may not believe this," our narrator tells us. "No one believes this; but it is true." Whether we believe it or not, we cannot avoid noticing that this strange sentence about the mutilation of a city's hills introduces us to a Christmas story about a boy who offers up, so to speak, his penis as a gesture of what the Catholic church used to call—and perhaps still calls—mortification of the flesh. Troubled by the stirrings of his genitals, he seeks castration. When he is denied it by the doctors, he undertakes to perform the operation himself. Not knowing what *castrate* means, however, he performs a more violent and dangerous operation on himself. What he does is not named, but the imprecise expressions "self-mutilated with a razor" and "amputation" leave little doubt about what he has done, even though it happens offstage and is reported elliptically through the conversation of the two doctors with the narrator. The text itself may be said to suffer from a certain mutilation, leaving the reader to supply its missing part, to name the operation that has come closer than any mere castration to a total change of sexuality.

Another ellipsis in the same story involves abortion. Dr. Fischer, who has refused to perform the castration, looks at his hands, "hands that had, with his willingness to oblige and his lack of respect for Federal statutes, made him his trouble" (*CSS*, 300). Again, the text will not quite name the trouble, but we are invited to infer that Dr. Fischer used to perform abortions. The symbol-hunters have been ready to point out that he is in fact a kind of Fischer king presiding over a wasteland named Kansas City. We have no doubt that Hemingway's allusion to T. S. Eliot's work is deliberate, but it makes sense only as part of a larger pattern that includes Constantinople. When Dr. Fischer refers to the boy as "the lad who sought eunuch-hood" (299) he invokes an archaic name for castration—a name, as it happens, that is historically associated with the Byzantine empire and with Constantinople itself. "The position of eunuchs in Byzantium was entirely different from that in the Arab countries or in Persia . . . for in Byzantium they often ran the government. In the sixth century, one of the greatest Byzantine generals was a eunuch. By the tenth century, eunuchs in the imperial court took precedence over non-eunuchs, and many of the most prominent men in both the state and the Church were eunuchs" (Bullough, 327). Hemingway may not have known all this, but he certainly associated Istanbul with castrations, as a casual remark in an attack upon literary critics demonstrates: "In the same way the Eunuch's Trade Journal and House Organ of Stamboul, Turkey gives little space and attention to the proprietors of the Harems. It is a tender subject" (K376a, 5–6). "God Rest You Merry, Gentlemen," then, also treats a tender subject, linking Kansas City, Constantinople, abortion, and castration. That is, it weaves together two places in which Hemingway lived and worked into a complex texture of history, analogy, metonymy and metaphor, linking them to the most powerful and violent denials of procreative activity known to humans. These are, in short, his places and his themes, deployed by leaving textual gaps, one of his favorite writing strategies.

The leaving of gaps precisely where sexual organs or actions must be named is elaborately connected, throughout Hemingway's work, with his fascinated attention to impotence, abortion, and sexual transgression. As we know, the word *abortion* is not used in "Hills Like White Elephants," a story whose title connects us to the mutilated hills of Kansas City and the mutilated (detusked) elephant in *The Garden of Eden*. No competent interpreter, so far as we know, wishes to deny that "Hills Like White Elephants" is about a projected abortion, but the name of the operation must indeed be inserted into a textual gap by the reader, just as the proper spelling of the venereal "malady" discussed in "One Reader Writes" must also be provided by a reader other than the one who writes in the story. All of Hemingway's readers must write, it seems, and the issues of reading and writing are regularly combined by him with matters of venery—and especially with the disasters, denials, and perversions of what he must have thought of as "normal" sexuality—a topic about which he did not write easily or well. Hemingway's best writing about sexuality involves divorce, castration, impotence, male and female homosexuality, transvestism, and transsexuality.

Many of these themes are taken up in "Mr. and Mrs. Elliot," the other story in which we have noted a perverse analogy to Kansas. This story was first called "Mr. and Mrs. Smith" because it was indeed about a Mr. and Mrs. Smith. Hemingway changed the names, as he changed the name of the heroine of "A Very Short Story" from Ag to Luz, to protect the guilty—namely himself—from possible lawsuits. The change to Elliot is usually interpreted as a slur against T. S. Eliot, whose name Hemingway regularly misspelled in this way. We agree that the allusion is to T. S. Eliot, but we don't think it is intended to be a personal slur quite as much as it is meant to invoke a puritan wasteland of impotence and sterility in which lesbian sexuality flourishes. We can approach that story by way of a passage in *The Sun Also Rises* singled out by Kenneth Lynn for discussion in his biography of Hemingway (1987). Lynn directs our attention to two ellipses in a scene in which Brett comforts Jake on his bed. She has arrived with Count Mippipopolous as Jake towels himself off after a shower. He goes into the bedroom to dress and is sitting there when Brett comes in. Lynn focuses on two moments in their conversation in which the word *then* seems to indicate an ellipsis in the narration. He argues that Brett must have provided Jake with some sort of sexual comfort during one of these ellipses after sending the count out on an errand. He claims to know just what Brett did, which we think is hardly justified, but we are prepared to accept his view that she did something that helped Jake feel better and that the something in question was probably erotic. This seems probable to us because it forms a pattern in Hemingway's work, one that operates in a similar way, for instance, in "Mr. and Mrs. Elliot."

The bland title does not reveal much, except that the story is about a married couple whose last name is significant enough to deserve mention in such a prominent place. It is a Yankee last name, even a Harvard name, perhaps a Puritan name—all of which will indeed prove meaningful. The tone of the narration is set in the first sentence: "Mr. and Mrs. Elliot tried very hard to have a baby." As a statement, this might call for sympathy. Most of us know people who have been in this position and we have regarded them with sympathy. But how often do we hear of people trying *hard* to have babies? Trying *very* hard? The most simple and direct effect of this intensification is to drain sympathy away from the Elliots' predicament and make them ludicrous. There is a secondary effect, however, in which the object of the satire is not the Elliots as individuals but the culture that has made procreation the sole legitimate object of sexual activity, transforming erotic play into alienated labor.

The second sentence seems to reveal how firmly Mrs. Elliot has internalized this cultural attitude: "They tried as often as Mrs. Elliot could stand it." It turns out, of course, that Mrs. Elliot is not without interest in sexual pleasures. She simply does not find them in heterosexual intercourse. In the first reading of this passage we are not so likely to leap to this perception, but in the long run the text will support this reading powerfully. In the first paragraph the emphasis is on sex as alienated labor, with the procreative effort taking on the quality of an assembly line: "They tried in Boston . . . and they tried . . . on the boat." Under this regime the Elliots' honeymoon becomes a *via dolorosa,* with a station of suffering for each new try in each new place.

The humor here, such as it is, is based on a binary opposition, deeply embedded in American culture, between puritan and libertine. In this instance the opposition takes the form of sex as sensual pleasure versus sex as procreative duty. In the "liberated" 1920s Hemingway was confident that his audience would share his perception that sex as a duty and burden must be ridiculous. This puritan-libertine opposition is invoked in other instances as well. A particularly telling passage is the description of Hubert Elliot's premarital experience: "He was twenty-five years old and had never gone to bed with a woman until he married Mrs. Elliot. He wanted to keep himself pure so that he could bring to his wife the same purity of mind and body that he expected of her. He called it to himself living straight. He had been in love with various girls before he kissed Mrs. Elliot and always told them sooner or later that he had led a clean life. Nearly all the girls lost interest in him" (*CSS,* 123). The explicitly puritanical character of Hubert's values is emphasized by the words *pure* and *purity.* In this narrative the code of purity is presented as absurd for the very good reason that girls are not interested in men who lack sexual experience. The American girl, in the view presented by this text, is far from being the virtuous, high-minded creature of sentimental literature. She is a practical, sensual person who is simply not interested in male purity.

Our concern in this story is the interaction—and occasional conflict—among the cultural codes invoked by the text. One such code emerges if we ignore Hubert Elliot's puritanism and study his values with a gaze adapted to more recent codes of sexual experience. Attending to the *structure* of his attitude toward women, as opposed to the merely sexual content of his utterances, we find him saying that "he wanted to . . . bring to his wife the same [condition] of mind and body that he expected of her" (123). To contemporary ears this seems like simple good sense, proposing a more genuinely fair and egalitarian attitude toward a woman than we can find in most of the male characters or narrators of *In Our Time*, including the narrator of this particular story. Our point is that the more obvious and powerful codes active in this text are those deployed by the knowing narrator, who shares the macho confidence usually attributed to the author. And to the extent that we share in the joke at the expense of Hubert Elliot and his wife, we accept those views, which are close to what is usually thought of as the Hemingway Code. But other codes are operating in this text, and they may lead us to another view of both this story and the larger Hemingway Text.

The sexual code is traversed in this story by several others that structure the flow of values and pleasure for the reader. One of these codes has to do with writing itself, for Hubert Elliot is a writer, "a poet with an income of nearly ten thousand dollars a year" (123). The casual delivery of these facts in the same clause seems to require interpretation. Why are they mentioned together? What have poetry and money to do with each other? No interpretation without a code! In this case the code seems to be based on a bohemian and romantic notion that the rich are not only barred from the Kingdom of Heaven but from the Province of Poetry as well. As one of us has argued in a previously (and obscurely) published essay, Hubert Elliot, whose initials are a reversal of Ernest Hemingway's, is indeed meant to be a reversed or inverted Hemingway figure. Hubert is a poet with an enormous income, Ernest a prose writer with a small one. Hubert writes "very long poems very rapidly," Ernest wrote very short stories (including "A Very Short Story," which appeared in the very same collection as Mr. and Mrs. Elliot") very slowly. Hubert paid in advance to have his work published (a datum that Hemingway inserted as an afterthought in the manuscript) while Ernest was paid for the stories he wrote. Hubert was inexperienced at sex and a prude, and Ernest—well, Ernest wanted to be the reverse of Hubert on that score and perhaps felt himself to be, but as Hadley, his first wife, later observed, "If Ernest had not been brought up in that damned stuffy Oak Park environment . . . he would not have thought that when you fall in love extramaritally, you have to marry the girl" (Kert, 226).

Our point is that Hemingway positioned Hubert Elliot to be his own opposite, but an opposite into whom he could project himself imaginatively, as he does in describing what he first called (in the "Smith" manuscript) "their wedding night": "They spent the night of the day they were married in a Boston hotel. They were both disappointed but finally Cornelia went to sleep. Hubert could not sleep and several times went out and walked up and down the corridor of the hotel in his new Jaeger bathrobe that he had bought for his wedding trip. As he walked he saw all the pairs of shoes, small shoes and big shoes, outside the doors of the hotel rooms. This set his heart to pounding and he hurried back to his own room but Cornelia was asleep. He did not like to waken her and soon everything was quite all right and he slept peacefully" (CSS, 124). This is a delightfully malicious image of the white hunter (Jaeger) prowling the corridors and having his dormant sexual potency aroused by the sight of heterosexual pairs of shoes, but even more malicious is the ellipsis in time marked by the "soon." Like the "then . . . and then" noticed by Kenneth Lynn in The Sun Also Rises, this "soon" directs our attention to a moment of sexual release that is not narrated. With Cornelia asleep, Hubert obtains his own relief, after which everything was quite all right. This is another of those textual gaps for which the reader must supply the missing sexual details—and this must is genuinely coercive. To get the point of the story the reader must fill the gap and, in effect, masturbate Hubert. Another angle on this theme and its embodiment in this particular story is provided by a manuscript fragment in which Hemingway began a list of books not published by the Three Mountains Press (Hemingway's Paris publisher). There are only two titles in this list. One of them is "Female Virgins and Male Masturbators/A study of intimate customs in the Puritan Commonwealth" (K613). Clearly Hemingway despised what he thought of as puritanism, just as he despised and wanted to humiliate the Ivy League poet on whom he based Hubert Elliot. But within this attitude we find another, in which Hemingway was aware of his own vestigial puritanism and of certain similarities between his own position and Hubert Elliot's. It is appropriate to see this characterization as, to a certain extent, Hemingway's attempt to objectify and distance a part of himself. Hubert is another version of the fear of impotence embodied in Jake Barnes—but a more malicious characterization, designed to establish Hemingway's own distance from this wealthy hack writer living in a ménage à trois: "Elliot had taken to drinking white wine and lived apart in his own room. He wrote a great deal of poetry during the night and in the morning looked very exhausted. Mrs. Elliot and the girl friend now slept together in the big mediaeval bed. They had many a good cry together. In the evening they all sat at dinner together in the garden under a plane tree and the hot evening wind blew and Elliot drank white wine and Mrs. Elliot and the girl friend made conversation and they were all quite happy" (*CSS*, 125). This is the same hot, dusty, wasteland wind that blew off the hills of Kansas City when it was like Constantinople. In this wasteland the writing of poetry has become equivalent to masturbation. (Hemingway added the phrase "and in the morning looked very exhausted" to the "Smith" manuscript so that we would not miss the analogy.) And having a good cry together has become equivalent to lesbian sexuality. Those tears will become an ocean in "The Sea Change," a story about a man whose beloved leaves him for another woman.

Sea Changes "The Sea Change" is a story in which it is shown that all red-blooded American girls do not necessarily want experienced men. Some of them prefer women. In "The Sea Change," a version of the material in "Mr. and Mrs. Elliot," the male protagonist is not so distanced from Ernest himself, nor is the woman so different from those Hemingway admired. In a manuscript draft of this story Hemingway stressed an element that was subdued in the published version but resurfaced, with a vengeance, in *The Garden of Eden*. This selection is from the first page of the manuscript: "It was the end of the summer and they were both tanned so that they looked out of place in Paris. The girl wore a tweed suit, her skin was a smooth gold brown, her blonde hair was cut short and ["the sun had varied the color"—crossed out in manuscript] grew beautifully away from her forehead. She had beautiful hands and her face and throat were tanned; her mouth was a little wide but a lovely shape and her cheek bones a little high but her face was handsome and her body slim. The man was very browned by the sun at the seashore. He was good looking too and he looked across the table at the girl" (K679, 1). Without undertaking a fuller reading of this passage, or of the story itself, we wish to point out a number of features with implications for the larger Hemingway Text. In this story about a woman leaving a man for another woman, we find a conspicuous mention of bobbed and bleached hair, of dark skin color, and of facial features that suggest some norm of beauty other than that of Western Europe or Anglo-America. Later in the same manuscript it is made plain that the young man's features are a mirror image of the young woman's: "His face was dark from the sun and his hair was dark but streaked by the sun a little too" (5). In a later manuscript version the story ends with the young man looking into the bar mirror, asking the bartender to serve him a drink: "What do the punks drink, James. What can you recommend to a recent convert? . . . Take a look at me and mix whatever you like." James tells the young man that he looks very good: "You have a fine tan." His response, and the final words of this fragment are, " 'I can see in the glass, James,' . . . 'I can see in the glass very clearly' " (K681). Since *punk* is a word used in Hemingway's world to designate male homosexuals, this version of the story suggests that the young woman's sea change of sexual preference has also changed the young man—or, rather, that he chooses ironically to distance his fear that this may be the case by naming it as he stares at his tanned face in the glass.

The title of the story comes from Ariel's speech in *The Tempest* about what happens to the bodies of drowned men, as every feature of their anatomies changes into "something rich and strange," a passage invoked by Eliot in *The Waste Land*. The change in Hemingway's story seems to have taken place by the sea also, where these two young people got their tans and their sun-bleached hair. This "sea change" material, including those lines not used in the published story, must have remained dormant in Hemingway's mind for decades before he was ready to tackle it on the scale of an entire novel. In the fifties, however, as he was working on the memoir of his Paris days, *A Moveable Feast,* these themes began to haunt him again. He deployed them, in the manuscript that was cleaned up and published as *The Garden of Eden,* in a fashion that took him deeper into his own obsessions than ever before.

Tribal Things *The Garden of Eden,* as one might expect from its title, is about the loss of innocence, especially the kind of innocence that is already sexual—but along lines that are innocently heteronomous with respect to gender and homogenous with respect to race. In the previous chapter we considered the way that metamorphosis or confusion of gender animates the characterization of Catherine Bourne. Now we shall explore how the theme of gender confusion and sexual exploration intersects with two other matters: desire for the racial "Other" and the search for aesthetic truth. What the unfinished text of *The Garden of Eden* is about, as we understand it, is the relation between a search for artistic "truth" and a sexuality that transgresses the norms of the culture that Hemingway kept trying to outgrow. Though it is not so visible in the sanitized version Scribners approved for publication, sexual "transgressions" in thought and deed become the keys that unlock the artist's sources of inspiration and allow him that glimpse of truth for which, as Joseph Conrad reminded us, the artist's public always forgets to ask— and, we might add, that it sometimes neglects to notice even when the gift is offered.

The full manuscript is about two couples, one consisting of a pair of painters, the other of a writer and his rich wife. The published version pretty well suppresses the painting pair, and we too shall ignore them this time. The other couple, as this version opens, are a newly married Adam and Eve of the 1920s celebrating their innocent love at a tiny village on the Mediterranean coast of the Camargue. The serpent in this French Eden is the wife, whose money and frustrated creative energies will ultimately destroy this paradise. In the published version this is clearly a fortunate fall, but the manuscript, including Hemingway's explicit instructions about the ending, seems aimed at something more complex and altogether darker. In both cases, however, the wife embodies the principle that will destroy this Eden. The text is not coy about this. David soon learns to call Catherine his "devil," and her "craziness," which is modeled on Hemingway's view of Zelda Fitzgerald's madness, becomes a topic of discussion as well. What the devil introduces into this Eden can be seen as a system of transgressive behavior in which a challenge to the norms of fashion or the social presentation of the body signifies, at a deeper level, an erotic transgression of boundaries of gender and race.

At the level of fashion and presentation of self, *The Garden of Eden* seems to be about the bobbing and dyeing of hair and the deep tanning of skin. It is plain, however, that these haircuts and dyeings are public signs of changes in sexuality. What is not so plain in the published book but is much clearer in the manuscript is that the darkening of skin color links this new eroticism to fantasies of miscegenation. We have already noted how bleached hair, tanned skin, and sexual changes are connected in "The Sea Change." This figure in the Hemingway carpet is part of an image repertoire that is woven and rewoven until it receives its fullest textual embodiment in *The Garden of Eden*. We can find it, for instance, in a fragmentary manuscript from the Parisian twenties in which a young man gets his hair cut on the rue de Faubourg St.-Honoré. The young man's face in a barber shop mirror shows "dark smooth healthy skin but no darker than a good healthy seashore tan." Sitting in the chair after asking for a permanent wave, he tries to avoid the glance of the young man in the next chair, whom he takes to be a pimp. When the other man gets up he revises his estimate: "I don't know a thing. Pimp hell. A joy spreader. He looked like a pimp in the chair. I thought he was a pimp. Just an upsidaisy. Why should I think he wasn't. Because I'm in here myself. Just like an upsidaisy. He looked at himself humorlessly in the mirror" (K355a, 5).

As in "The Sea Change," we have a man looking in a mirror, concerned about contamination by association with homosexuality. And again we find homoeroticism textually connected to hair dressing and skin tanning. The dark skin of the young man in this story, however, is not really tanned; Aldo Lombardo is dark because he is an Italian—he was born in Vicenza and grew up in Chicago—which means that the reference to tanning at the seashore and a later reference to the appearance in the mirror of "his face tanned" is gratuitous with respect to the story and therefore more thoroughly motivated by its sources in Hemingway's own image repertoire. The point is that Lombardo could have been described simply as dark or swarthy without any analogy to the artificial sea change of tanning, but the influence of the larger Hemingway Text, a network of images and values built up over his lifetime, is apparent in this fragment.

Emerging from this larger hidden text are fragmentary manuscripts that weave together race, eroticism, and madness. Writing of his second meeting with the Fitzgeralds in the appropriately named Dingo Bar (dingoes are aboriginal dogs), Hemingway noted that "the only thing beautiful about her [Zelda] was the tawny smoothness of her skin, the lovely color of her hair, which had been ruined in texture by an unsuccessful permanent wave, and her legs which were wonderful; light and long as nigger legs. . . . I did not like her but that night I had an erotic enough dream about her. The next time I saw her I told her that and she was pleased" (K486, 9). In an early draft of the story "Fathers and Sons," Nick Adams' Ojibway girlfriend ("who did first what no one has ever done better") is described as having "thin brown legs" (K382). In the version published in *Winner Take Nothing* these legs have been plumped up (*NAS*, 266), but this manuscript, coupled with the sketch of Zelda Fitzgerald, enables us to see the connection in Hemingway's larger Text between eroticism and dark slender legs, whether they be African ("nigger legs") or Native American ("thin brown legs"). In the manuscript for *The Garden of Eden* this connection is developed and complicated by the motif of sexual transformation and transgression.

These transformations and transgressions begin early in the published novel, when Catherine Bourne returns from her trip to Aigues-Mortes (Still Waters or, perhaps, Dead Sea) with her hair "cropped as short as a boy's" (*GofE*, 14–15). This "devil" then initiates changes in the couple's sexual encounters that Hemingway does not describe specifically but which the text encourages us to imagine as imitations of homoerotic embraces or heteroerotic ones in which each partner has assumed the other's sex. It is Catherine who is setting the pace in these sexual experiments, though not, as becomes clearer and clearer, merely as an erotic game but because she is losing her grip on reality. The experiments, in short, are dangerous because they are tapping into something powerfully irrational, something primitive and savage.

The obsession with tanning is connected with the desire to reach a primal level of experience, some heart of darkness, from which Euro-Americans have been cut off by their heritage of enlightenment. In Chapter 3, when David asks Catherine how far she is planning to carry the darkening of her skin, she replies that she intends to get as "dark as I can. We'll see. I wish I had some [Kanaka or—in manuscript] Indian blood" (31). This passage has been heavily worked over by the editor of the published book. The suppression of the reference to Kanaka blood is just the beginning of the expurgative effort. In the manuscript Catherine's speech continues this way: "It's the changing that is as important as the dark. But I'm going to be so dark you won't be able to stand it and you'll be helpless. White women will always bore you. I can't wait to go to the beach tomorrow" (K422.1–2, chap. 4, p. 3).

After Catherine goes to sleep in this scene David muses about what they have been doing. Once again, because the published text has been heavily expurgated, we must quote from the manuscript that stands behind page 31 of the printed book:

> She changes from a girl into a boy and back to a girl carelessly and happily and she enjoys corrupting me and I enjoy being corrupted.

But she's not corrupt and who says it is corruption? I withdraw the word. Now we are going to be a special dark race of our own with our own pigmentation, [and we already have our own tribal customs—crossed out in manuscript] growing that way each day as some people would garden or plant and raise a crop. The trouble with that is that it will not grow at night too. It can only be made in the sun, in strong sun against the reflection of the sand and the sea. So we must have the sun to make this sea change. The sea change was made in the night and it grows in the night and the darkness that she wants and needs now grows in the sun." (K422.1/2, chap. 4, p. 4)

As this passage makes entirely explicit, tanning—a darkness caused by sunlight reflected by sea and sand—is the external sign of the sea change worked internally by the dark tribal deeds of night.

The process described here is a metamorphic shift of race and gender. The nature of this change is elaborated and complicated in the manuscript by deliberate reference to works of plastic art in which the theme of metamorphosis is explicit. The first and most important of these is the sculpture by Rodin that was called, among other things, *The Metamorphoses*. The statue is first invoked by Catherine as she and David are in bed after dinner in Le Grau du Roi. The mention has been excised from page 17 of the published book, after her words "Please understand and love me":

"Do you remember the sculpture in the Rodin museum?"
"Which one?"
"That one."
"Yes."
"Now try and be good and not think and only feel. Can you see me?"
"Only just see you."

"Don't think," she said. "Don't think at all."

He lay back and did not think at all.

"Are you changing like in the sculpture?"

"No."

"Are you trying to?"

"No."

After a brief passage that elliptically describes their new erotic muta-
tion, ending with Catherine's question, "Now you can't tell who is who,
can you?" and David's reply, "No," the manuscript continues:

"Now we are the way it is?"

"Yes."

"Now will you please be that way now? Will you? Will you? Will you
please?"

"How?"

"Will you change and be my girl and let me take you? Will you be like
you were in the statue? Will you change?"

He knew now and it was like the statue. The one there are no
photographs of and of which no reproductions are sold.

"You are changing," she said. "Oh you are. You are. Yes you are and
you're my girl Catherine." (K422.1/1, 21)

What is at stake here for David Bourne is not just the breaking of a
sexual taboo but the loss of his own identity as a heterosexual male.
What may make it worth his while to risk this stake is the possibility of
breaking into new aesthetic territory, which for him, as for Hemingway,
means being able to reach a deeper level of truth. The lesbian eroticism
of Rodin's *Metamorphoses* clearly fascinated Hemingway, but so did
the idea of gender metamorphosis itself. In this respect he belongs with
other modernists like T. S. Eliot, whose Tiresias, an "old man with
wrinkled dugs," is presented as a key to the modern experience. What is

different about Hemingway's appropriation of gender metamorphosis is that it combines with racial metamorphosis.

Hemingway once joked about grinding up T. S. Eliot into powder and sprinkling it on Joseph Conrad's grave to bring the writer of *The Heart of Darkness* back to life. He is actually doing something like that in *The Garden of Eden*. The truth David Bourne wants to find lies in Africa, an undiscovered country whose bourne he must reach in whatever way he can. Thus the narrative moves from transgression to transgression, metamorphosis to metamorphosis, closer and closer to Africa. The metamorphosis begun in France is continued in Spain, where this transgressive eroticism brings David to the point of deep remorse, in which concern about his own honor is blended with worry about Catherine's inability to confine her sexual transformations to the bedroom.

The trip to Madrid is important because it allows for the textual weaving together of erotic primal scenes and the "dark continent" itself. In a conversation preserved in the published novel, Catherine remarks that she has heard some clever person say that "Africa begins at the Pyrenees" (*GofE*, 52). David replies that it is more complicated than that but that "once you're in from the coast [Spain] gets to be Africa fast enough." In Madrid (which is, of course, well in from the coast) Catherine, with her boyish bob and her deeply tanned skin, seems to become more African. Colonel Boyle observes, for instance, that she is "the darkest white girl I've ever seen" (63). The colonel also describes her appearance as he observed her looking at artworks in the Prado, where she might have been "the young chief of a warrior tribe who had gotten loose from his councillors and was looking at that marble of Leda and the Swan" (62). Here the colonel not only describes Catherine as male (a chief) but as African (a warrior tribe) and as contemplating a visual text of miscegenation across species lines: bird and woman, a nice complement to a dream Hemingway once had of copulating with a lioness: "In my nocturnal dreams I am always between the age of 25 or 30 years old, I am irresistible to women, dogs and on one recent occasion a very beautiful lioness.

"In the dream this lioness, who became my fiancée, was one of the most delightful creatures I have ever dreamt about. She had some of the characteristics of Miss Mary and she could become irascible. On one occasion I recall she did an extremely perilous act. Perilous to me that is" (K332a, 41).

Miscegenation across species lines is erotic in itself in the Hemingway Text, but it is also a metaphor for racial miscegenation, which had a special eroticism for Hemingway. In the statue of Leda that Catherine was seen contemplating, transgressive eroticism is linked with metamorphosis as it is in the Rodin. The Prado has only one Leda and the Swan, a copy of a fourth-century B.C. sculpture attributed to Timotheos. It is a figure of about life-size in which Leda is seated and holding the rather small swan on her lap. The myth has many variations, but this statue is animated by a version in which Zeus has changed himself into a swan in order to approach Leda, the chaste wife of Tyndareus. His approach is aided in that, as a swan, he seems in great danger from a pursuing eagle, possibly his own familiar bird assisting in his sexual endeavor. At any rate, as a swan, Zeus takes refuge from his pursuer on Leda's lap. (Most of us, conditioned by Yeats's version of the story, imagine a large bird engaged in a brutal rape, but many artists have seen the affair quite differently, including, apparently, Timotheos.) In the Prado version the sculptor has positioned Leda at a crucial moment: she has just caught sight of the eagle above her and, leaving herself naked, she is raising her cloak to hide the swan from the eagle while the wily bird snuggles between her unprotected legs. The Prado is not noted for its classical collection, but Hemingway must have known it well enough to choose deliberately to associate Catherine with this particular plastic text of erotic transgression. It is also worth noting that among the museum's modest collection of classical sculpture, which Catherine could scarcely have avoided encountering because they are displayed near the Leda, are a number of hermaphrodites and other figures of ambiguous sexuality. In any case, the detail of Catherine's examination of "that marble of Leda and the Swan" extends and enriches the text's codes of miscegenation and sexual metamorphosis. It is not only what she sees that counts in this instance, however, but what she looks like when she is seeing it.

In the image of Catherine as warrior chief contemplating the sculpture Hemingway has woven together the classical themes of gender change and erotic transgression with a primal space represented by Africa—Spain as Africa and the African warrior chief in Spain). Much later, Marita, the third member of the erotic triangle that will spring up in this Garden of Eden, will be described in the manuscript as looking like "a young native warrior of a good tribe under interrogation, to be followed, probably, by torture" (K422.1/20, 12). In this case Catherine is doing the questioning and Marita is being interrogated. At different moments in this text, then, each of these women is represented as a male African warrior, with the change of sex and change of race erotically linked to metamorphosis and rape or interrogation and torture. As this ménage à trois is established in the novel, each partner pairs off at one time or another with one of the others, but Catherine's lesbian encounter with Marita is a disaster, another stage in Catherine's disintegration. For Marita, however, who was in a lesbian relationship when she met the Bournes, her night with Catherine is just a stage in her conversion to heterosexuality by David, who is allowed by Hemingway to play out the familiar male fantasy of converting a lesbian to another way of sexuality—a bit of wish fulfillment that attempts to allay or negate the anxieties of "The Sea Change" and "Mr. and Mrs. Elliot."

There is no question that, in the character of Marita, Hemingway indulged himself as he did with his contessa in *Across the River and into the Trees*. Marita is the perfect writer's spouse—smart, sexy, submissive, and appreciative of his work rather than jealous of it. But there is more to it than that, something that links *The Garden of Eden* to a deeper level of the Hemingway Text than *Across the River*. At this level, eroticism, race, and creative truth are connected, though the connection between eroticism and race that runs throughout the manuscript was largely erased from the published text. It is especially visible, for instance, in a conversation that occurs while the the three lovers are tanning after a swim (K422.1/17, 23–25). Catherine tells Marita that David once nearly married "a beautiful Oklahoma oil Indian squaw," which leads to a discussion of tanning as a way of changing racial identity. Urging Marita to get darker, Catherine says, "You'd be better with that dark walnut color I was at first. . . . When I was a Kanaka. Now I'm working to be Somali." This leads to a discussion of Somali women, in which Catherine asks whether it is true "that Somali women have ways of holding a man so he can never leave them."

David says that it has happened that way and goes on to suggest that they have been especially successful with white men because "they treat them like they know Somali men really like to be treated and the men think they're the first person this ever happened to." Later, in a passage suppressed from what is page 185 of the published novel, Marita soliloquizes while fondling the private parts of the sleeping David: "Maybe it will make him have a lovely dream, she thought. Maybe he will dream he's back in Africa and his first girl is playing with him or his Somali girl. I know what she did and I'll do that too. He liked it when I did it before. The time before we ever made love. I'll do that now too while he's asleep but not to make anything happen just softly and gently so he won't even know but think it is a dream. . . . I can do the other thing the thing she told me about Madrid better than she can because I can be it better" (K422.1/27, 32–33).

Erotic fantasies about race change and sex change are continually brought together in this text. As the conversation on the beach about Somali women continues, the subject shifts to Somali men:

"Are Somali men different?
"Sure."
"Are they anything like you?"
"Not much but maybe a little."
"Like me now?"
"Yes." (K422.1/17, 25)

The last three lines were crossed out by Hemingway in the manuscript, but the subject that has emerged from the creative process here—that of Catherine turning into not merely a Somali woman but a Somali man— surfaces in other parts of the text as well. Here, however, the author turns the conversation back to women, and it concludes with both Catherine and Marita vowing to be good "Somali wives" to David.

There is much talk in the novel about going to Africa, first between David and Catherine and later between David and Marita, but "going to Africa" comes to have a sexual as well as geographical meaning, as in this conversation between David and Marita:

"I'm going to do the Africa thing."
"Don't try and make yourself like a Wakamba or M'Bulu girl."
"I'm going to be better than that."
"We'll go to Africa."
"We'll have Africa tonight." (K422.1/35, 29)

When Marita suggests that she and David could do what Catherine and David had done in Madrid, only without remorse, she adds, in a line that Hemingway crossed out, "We both have a darker side than anyone. A truly dark side" (K422.1/35, 32). Later in the manuscript Marita has her hair cropped so that she looks like "a close sheared beaver" or like a "Bizerte street urchin" with hair like a "water-front arab's" (K422.1/36, 1). In this passage Marita is clearly presented as having both an African identity and an animal one. Like the lioness Hemingway dreamed of, Marita has her catlike dimension:

> "I'm proud of you and you look wonderful."
> "Stroke once so I can purr."
> "Can you purr?"
> "I've been purring ever since we did it." (K422.1/36, 3)

Talking over her new appearance with David, Marita says that she wanted to look like his African girl, the young Somali woman who was his "fiancée." David replies that she does indeed "look like Africa," but "very far north and you mixed up the genders" (2):

> "I wish I could have been exactly like your African girl."
> "You're better."
> "I don't want to be better. I want to be worse and I want to be your boy too."
> "No."
> "Yes I will be and you'll love it and never have remorse." (4)

Things go on in this vein, with Marita insisting that "I'm your street arab and I love it. I wanted to be your Mbulu girl. But after all you did have an Mbulu girl. But you never had what I am. Not even in Madrid" (K422.1/36, 25). Finally, David and Marita do indeed replicate the Madrid experience, which David has written about in a journal that Marita read. In her Molly Bloomish flow of posterotic thought she muses, "I wish we could have gone to sleep still that way. But then he would have had remorse. I'm sure he would. Later he won't I think. He loves it as much as I do. . . . I'd never known until I read the part about Madrid. . . . He'd never have known if Catherine hadn't done it to him. . . . No wonder it's forbidden. We must have the same tribal things. We don't have to go by any Hebrew laws or tabus" (K422.1/36, 35).

It was after David's first experience of dark sexuality in Madrid, and after Marita joined him and Catherine, that he was able to finish his first story since their marriage, a story of Africa and his loss of innocence there (*GofE*, 108). In the manuscript he muses to himself about the relation between his life and his writing: "If you live by the senses you will die by them and if you live by your invention and your head you will die by that too. All that is left entire in you is your ability to write and that gets better. You would think it would be destroyed. By everything you have been taught it should. But so far as you corrupt or change that grows and strengthens. It should not but it has" (K422.1/17, 9). And later, "All that you know is that you have written better, clearer, and *plus net*, he used the French phrase in thinking, as you have deteriorated morally" (9bis). Later, after Catherine has burned these manuscripts, his ability to rewrite them is unleashed by the recapitulation of Madrid staged by Marita in her guise of street Arab. After their night of "Africa" David begins writing in the morning, recaptures his power as a writer, and emerges from his writing room looking like a "great animal," a racehorse named "Heros XII." Turning to Marita he says, "You broke me loose." She replies, "We broke each other loose" (K422.1/37, 10).

This exchange means that her erotic performance has brought David once again into that imaginative territory—call it Africa—in which he can reach his fictional truth. Originally, David broke into new imaginative territory because of his sexual transgressions with Catherine. But because Catherine could not negotiate the passage between imagination and reality and between her sexual roles and her gender, and because of

David's remorse, this breakthrough was only partially successful. Later, with Marita, these sexual transgressions seem to have no such prices attached, partly because they are more fully imaginative, more consciously and deliberately performed. At least that is the conclusion Hemingway seems to have been reaching for, but he either could not textualize or did not live to textualize completely this dimension of his thought. His own puritanism, perhaps, the Hubert Elliot in himself that he never quite transcended and which was one of his imaginative strengths, asserted itself again.

Just as David is presented as having broken loose from an orthodox heterosexuality, first guided by Catherine and then by Marita, Marita herself is presented as having been freed from what might be called an orthodox lesbianism. Now they both have entered an erotic dream world in which race and gender are changed by "tribal" rituals. David's writing, of course, is *about* Africa, about his youth there and, in the story that we are allowed to read, about shame. This tale of the elephant hunt is a story about separation from the father, just as David's new erotic experiences are about the rejection of "Hebrew laws or tabus." The published novel allows only part of this story to appear, conveying the impression by its omissions that Marita has restored David to a more "normal" erotic life, whereas the manuscript indicates that it is precisely the "abnormality" of their relationship that has refreshed and renewed his creative energies.

The published novel also offers this sanitized relationship as a happy ending in which innocence has been recaptured and the serpent Catherine banished so that Eden may be Eden once again. As we see it, however, Hemingway was torn between a more complex and African happy ending, on the one hand, and a version in which happiness is permanently out of reach. In the happier version we have a tale in which the truth about the loss of innocence can be discovered only by one who keeps alive the experience of losing it, and Africa can be found only by establishing one's own erotic tribal rituals. The more somber ending, closer to that of *The Sun Also Rises* than to the published text of *The Garden of Eden,* is the one that he drafted and left with instructions to use if he did not live to finish the novel. In the "Provisional Ending" (K422.2/1) Catherine and David have returned to the Riviera some considerable time after their Edenic experience there. What has become of Marita we do not know. But Catherine has, presumably, gone through some sort of mental rehabilitation in a Swiss clinic. She asks if David remembers "when we were both virginal in Madrid," and he answers, "I remember Madrid." Later she observes, "You can't take the sun much anymore, can you?" (2). And finally, "We didn't go to Africa. It was too much like Spain." David answers, "We went to Africa" (5).

To those for whom Hemingway is an interesting writer because his simple surfaces regularly allow glimpses into unresolved anxieties in our own lives, our own hopes and fears, the Scribners text of this novel does its author a serious disservice, and the publisher's ending is truly unfortunate. Although the editors used their blue pencils on some turgid prose that Hemingway himself might ultimately have rejected, they surely went too far in concealing the darkness of this text, with its equivocal but genuine endorsement of transgressive eroticism and its fascination with a truth that can be found only by penetrating to the heart of a dark erotic continent called Africa. Hemingway's admiration for Conrad is well known. Surely he intended in this work to give us one of those glimpses of truth for which, as Conrad reminded us in the preface to *The Nigger of the Narcissus,* we regularly forget to ask. It is, then, a great pity that Scribners has treated us as if we were Kurtz's "Intended" instead of allowing us to come to grips with the complexity of sea changes and tribal things in Hemingway's unfinished novel.

4 Toros, Cojones, y Maricones

Maricón: a sodomite, nance, queen, fairy, fag, etc. They have these in Spain too, but I only knew of two of them among the forty-some matadors de toros. This is no guaranty that those interested parties who are continually proving that Leonardo da Vinci, Shakespeare, etc. were fags would not be able to find more. Of the two, one is almost pathologically miserly, is lacking in valor but is very skillful and delicate with the cape, a sort of exterior decorator of bullfighting, and the other has a reputation for great valor and awkwardness and has been unable to save a peseta. In bullfighting circles the word is used as a term of opprobrium or ridicule or as an insult. There are many very, very funny fairy stories.

—"Explanatory Glossary," *Death in the Afternoon*

It is not every writer on bullfighting who feels obliged to have an entry on homosexuality in the glossary. But Hemingway is no ordinary writer on bullfighting or on anything else. In this chapter we look into what seems to us an extraordinary interest in homoeroticism on Hemingway's part, and an unusual way of writing about it. Even his definition of maricón is far from ordinary.

It is obvious by the tone of the definition (the use of the word *fags*, for instance, added after the first draft) that Hemingway wants to distance himself from those he is writing about here (the "fairy stories" are "*very, very* funny"), but it is also obvious that he has taken enough interest in the topic to count the number of gay blades among the practicing matadors and has come up with a figure of two out of forty-some, or roughly 5 percent. In 1931 who else was counting the number of homosexual males in any sport or contest of life and death? Beyond that, his descriptions of the two bullfighters who are maricones are especially interesting. One is miserly, graceful, and cowardly, and the other is spendthrift, clumsy, and brave. Both men are described in terms of the same three qualities—and each man is the opposite of the other on all three counts. The result of this is to counter the kind of statement often made by Hemingway himself or by one of his characters to the effect that it is easy to tell homosexual males by some quality that they all have in common. From Hemingway's glossary entry, then, we learn that homosexuals can be brave or cowardly, graceful or clumsy, miserly or spendthrift—like everybody else. In the manuscript of the glossary (K25), the comparison of the two bullfighters did not attend to the economic dimension, nor did the later typescript (K35). Hemingway kept working on this entry, expanding it with every version up to the proofs. These continual revisions proclaim Hemingway's continuing interest in the topic, and they also reveal that, as he extended his comparison, he deliberately continued contrasting his two exemplary maricones on every point. His final attention to their handling of money can be connected to other instances in which he suggests that male homosexuals are careful with money. But he introduces this identifying characteristic only to undo it by assigning its opposite to the other bullfighting maricón.

One of the startling features of Hemingway's writing is that most of his fictional bullfighters—with the exception of Romero in *The Sun Also Rises*—appear to be versions of one or the other of this pair of exceptions to the rule of heterosexuality. That is, they are either graceful, cowardly, and tight with money, or brave, clumsy, and poor. How many of them are also maricones is less clear. It is certainly the case that the first long stories Hemingway wrote about bullfighting are about two matadors who closely conform to the glossary descriptions. Gavira in the never-finished "A Lack of Passion" is cowardly, an artist with the cape, and called a maricón twice by the waitress Inès in a fragment of the unfinished text (Beegel, 93); while Manolo, in "The Undefeated," is clumsy, brave, and penniless, though his sexuality is not specifically indicated. We shall return to these stories, but for now it is enough to notice that the framework of the bullring and its culture allowed Hemingway to attend to many aspects of male homosocial desire (to borrow Eve Sedgwick's term), specifically including genitally oriented desire.

The connection between male sexuality and bullfighting is made repeatedly in the Hemingway Text. The glossary "OF CERTAIN WORDS, TERMS AND PHRASES USED IN BULLFIGHTING" (379) includes all three of the Spanish nouns mentioned in the title of this chapter. Not only is maricón a necessary term, so is *cojones*: "testicles; a valorous bullfighter is said to be plentifully equipped with these. In a cowardly bullfighter they are said to be absent. Those of the bull are called *criadillas* and prepared in any of the ways sweetbreads are usually cooked they are a great delicacy. During the killing of the fifth bull the criadillas of the first bull were sometimes served in the royal box. Primo de Rivera was so fond of interlarding his discourse with reference to manly virtues that he was said to have eaten so many criadillas that they had gone to his brain" (396).

Many commentators are apparently of the opinion that Hemingway, too, may have eaten too many criadillas, but his very ability to mock this excessive attention to manly virtues should discourage us from too quickly applying this criterion to Hemingway himself. We suggest that, on the contrary, the connection between bulls and manliness, already present in the textuality of Spain itself, was appropriated by Hemingway in a manner that allowed him to explore aspects of manliness, including male desire directed toward other males, to an extent that no other cultural context available to him could have provided. In his *traje de luces* (suit of lights) a bullfighter is on display in a bejeweled garment that both conceals and reveals his body, including his sexual organs. And, in its traditional practice, bullfighting was a skill that required both the grace of a dancer and the attitude of a killer. For Hemingway, as for others who wrote about it, it was an art rather than a sport, and it made sense to speak of it in terms like *classic* and *decadent,* which are drawn from the vocabulary of aesthetics. It was also necessary then, or Hemingway found it so, to speak of a veronica as a "pass with the cape so called because the cape was originally grasped in the two hands in the manner in which Saint Veronica is shown in religious paintings to have held the napkin with which she wiped the face of Christ" (*DIA,* 459–60)—just as necessary as it was to speak of the testicular attributes of both bulls and bullfighters. Bullfighting, then, became a pretext for interests that Hemingway could scarcely have expressed without that pretextual excuse. The entry on cojones, as it happens, was not in Hemingway's manuscript of the glossary but was added in the typescript (K35) and extended after that. But Hemingway's interest in genital matters was not confined to the main text of the book or to the glossary.

The first of the extensive collection of photographs included in *Death in the Afternoon* is not a picture of a matador nor of a fighting bull. It is titled "THE SEED BULL" (Hemingway wrote the titles and captions himself), and we are instructed in the caption to notice the loins, "where eight hundred and twenty-two sons came from to the ring" (281). A father who has sent more than eight hundred sons to certain death is an interesting specimen indeed of patriarchal practice, with a ponderous body that has become, in the words of the text, "the bull's own monument." The word *toro* is as rich in genital connotations, then, as the other two words in our chapter title.

The usual view of Hemingway's interest in sexuality is that it is of the locker-room sort, kidding-with-the-guys but fiercely heterosexual in its focus, treating homosexuality as either a joke or a horror. We do not want to imply that this view is entirely wrong; there is indeed a locker-room joker in the Hemingway Text. But there is also someone else, someone denied but presupposed by that very mentality. The locker-room viewpoint may be found in the many places in Hemingway's writing where male homosexuality is coded as a form of femininity that deforms the male body and makes it repulsive to an eye oriented to an essence of manliness that excludes everything female. But the Hemingway Text does not always speak of this pure vision of masculinity or in a single macho voice. Even the phallic (or, perhaps better, cojonic) text of *Death in the Afternoon* has a way of sliding into the mariconic. In one passage, the topic of homosexuality appears almost by accident, it seems, and then it proceeds to take over the discourse. The passage begins as a discussion of Spanish painting, which is itself tacked on to a chapter on the art of placing the banderillas: "Do you want conversation? What about? Something about painting?" (203). This passage was added in typescript to the galley proofs of *Death in the Afternoon,* in which the question about conversation had originally been answered in the negative, bringing the chapter to a close (galley 60 and typed manuscript, "Insert A," K49 and K50). In proposing to discuss painting, Hemingway asks, "Something to please Mr. Huxley?"

Aldous Huxley entered this book about bullfighting a few pages previously, in a section that was added to the preceding chapter (chapter 16) after the typed draft was complete. In an essay called "Foreheads Villainous Low" Huxley had ventured to use an example from Hemingway's *A Farewell to Arms* to illustrate the notion that his fellow writers were ashamed of being "cultured" in the sense of being "clever, cultivated, interested in the things of the mind" (Huxley, 202). The example, which Hemingway quoted at some length in chapter 16, was a citation of what Huxley referred to as " 'the bitter nail-holes' of Mantegna's Christs,' " after which, he observed, "appalled by his own temerity, the author passes on" (201).

Huxley's quotation is not exact, and Hemingway knew it. He also knew that in the passage cited—a conversation between Catherine and Frederic—other artists are mentioned. But he took up Huxley in chapter 16 to introduce a literary discussion of the need to make characters in books talk as people actually talk—part of his point being that you should not accuse the author of cultural timidity when he is not writing as himself but writing the conversation of people in his books. He returns to Huxley at the end of chapter 17, however, to take up the other part of his challenge—to speak, in his own voice, about art. The last-minute inclusion of this discussion with the corrected galley proofs indicates that Huxley's criticism had continued to bother Hemingway to the point where he felt required to respond more directly.

Beyond this direct reply, however, we want to postulate a more indirect reply to other aspects of the book in which Huxley's essay appeared, *Music at Night and Other Essays* (1931), which Hemingway owned and packed in crate No. 20 when he left Key West for Cuba in 1940 (Reynolds 1981, 65). As we understand it, the challenge that Hemingway decided to take up in chapter 17 was twofold. In the title essay of his volume, Huxley himself took a stab at writing about two Madonnas by way of showing that there is not much that can usefully be said about a work of art "in one's own words." That is, he did his best to write a comparison of "a Virgin by Piero della Francesca with a Virgin by Tura" (48) and then concluded that no one's best would be very good, unless it were that of "philosophers or literary artists who find it convenient to make the criticism of other men's work a jumping off place for their own creativity" (51).

Huxley followed this essay, however, with one called "Meditation on El Greco," in which he tried to account for the mysterious power of El Greco's work, taking as his key to this power a strange image from an early painting by El Greco called *The Dream of Philip II*. It is clear that Huxley was using the painting as a jumping off place for his own creativity, which he demonstrated partly by choosing a corner of the painting on which to focus his interest and partly by the manner in which he discussed this corner. The image Huxley chose to focus on was that of "a vast concourse, presumably of the damned" hurrying down the "crimson throat" of a whale (55). "Whither are they bound, those hastening damned? 'Down the red lane,' as our nurses used to say when they were encouraging us to swallow the uneatable viands of childhood. Down the red lane into an inferno of tripes. Down, in a word, into that strange and rather frightful universe which Greco's spirit seems to have come more and more exclusively, as he grew older, to inhabit. For in the Cretan's later painting every personage is a Jonah" (56–57). Huxley went on in this vein (which we assure you will be significant when we come to consider Hemingway's view of the same artist) for some pages, insisting that El Greco turned spiritual matters into physiological ones: "The symbols of the spiritual open spaces are compelled by him to serve as a language in terms of which he talks about the immediacies of visceral awareness, about the ecstasy that annihilates the personal soul, not by dissolving it out into universal infinity, but by drawing it down and drowning it in the warm, pulsating, tremulous darkness of the body. . . . If El Greco had somewhere specifically told us what he meant to convey by painting in terms of Black Holes and mucus, I should not now be in a position to speculate. But luckily he never told us; I am justified in letting my fancy loose to wander" (67–68).

One might observe that El Greco is functioning here somewhat in the manner of a Rorschach blot and that it is Huxley who is preoccupied with Black Holes and mucus and the warm, pulsating, tremulous darkness of the body rather than the Cretan, as he occasionally calls the painter. But Huxley's fantasy proved very powerful. Henry Miller took it up as a metaphor for the writing of Anaïs Nin in an essay on her work that appeared in *The Criterion* magazine and again in Miller's *Max and the White Phagocytes*. And George Orwell took it from Miller to use as a metaphor for the writing of Miller himself and the thirties in general in his famous essay "Inside the Whale." For our purposes, however, what is important is that Hemingway could not resist responding to this vision either, though his response was not to borrow but to transform.

We believe, then, that Huxley's "Meditation on El Greco" is a major pretext for the conversation on art that Hemingway added at the end of chapter 17 of *Death in the Afternoon*.

Self-consciously noting that he could put in something to make the book "worthwhile" because "this is the end of a chapter," Hemingway moved quickly from Huxley to the German art historian Julius Meier-Graefe, who had visited Spain in 1911 and written a book about his travels. "When Julius Meier-Graefe, the German critic, came to Spain he wanted to see the Goyas and Velasquezes to have publishable ecstasies about them, but he liked the Grecos better. He was not content to like Greco better; he had to like him alone, so he wrote a book proving what poor painters Goya and Velasquez were in order to exalt Greco, and the yardstick that he chose to judge these painters by was their respective paintings of the crucifixion of Our Lord" (203). Hemingway owned the relevant book by Meier-Graefe, *A Spanish Journey* (which he had also borrowed from Silvia Beach's bookstore in the winter of 1926–27), packing a copy of it in crate No. 17 when bound for Cuba in 1940 (Reynolds 1981, 63, 158). And he is reasonably accurate about the general drift of Meier-Graefe's book. But the book had relatively little to say about Goya, and Hemingway knew this. His first rough beginning of this discussion of Meier-Graefe's book mentioned only Velasquez and El Greco (K63). Hemingway introduced Goya presumably because of his own strong interest in that painter, about whom he intended to publish a short ecstasy near the end of this chapter himself. But one of the German art historian's brief discussions of Goya was undoubtedly useful to Hemingway in a way he was less ready to acknowledge. Goya's *Disasters of War* is one of the many texts that stand behind Hemingway's essay "A Natural History of the Dead," which appears in chapter 12 of *Death in the Afternoon*. Goya is mentioned in that essay, but what is not mentioned is that Meier-Graefe, in *The Spanish Journey*, had discussed one of the sketches for Goya's war series in a manner that must have stimulated Hemingway's own thinking about the representation of death in war. Here is Meier-Graefe's discussion:

> In the Taubmann collection there is a sketch of Goya's which belongs to the group of his *Desastros de la Guerra*. After the manner of the Cucana in the Berlin National Gallery, but far smaller, and, if possible, even more beautiful. Incomparably more lovely than anything that I have yet seen of Goya. It is a monumental scene of incredible reality within the space of the width of your hands. Corpses at the foot of a mountainous village in the grey of dawn. The sinister element for once does not depend upon the concept of the corpse. Nor is it a collection of particularly grotesque or picturesque bodies. But it is a field of dead men. The tones of the bodies combine with those of the earth; the design—a liquid and modelling stroke of the brush of the greatest rapidity—represents the bodies simultaneously as the height and depth of the ground. It thus happens that the whole earth seems, as it were, covered with corpses, and one gains the impression of a kind of vegetation of dead men, an uncanny life in death. (77–78)

Hemingway had of course written about the dead often before this particular essay, and, indeed, he recycled some of his earlier material here, as his interlocutor, the Old Lady, tells him indignantly. But the idea of treating the dead precisely in terms of natural history seems to have been stimulated by Meier-Graefe's reading of Goya's sketch, just as the idea of taking the dead as a subject for art was certainly supported by Goya's own work. It is this connection, complex as it is, that helps to account for and integrate this sketch of the military dead into a book about another way of dying in broad daylight. And just as Meier-Graefe, in his book about painting, has some passages about bullfighting, Hemingway, in his book about bullfighting, has some passages about painting. Spain and its deadly arts provide the possibility—perhaps the necessity—for this particular mixture of topics.

We should note that Hemingway is grossly unfair in charging that Meier-Graefe based his comparisons exclusively or even mainly on paintings of crucifixions. Only once—and not until his book was nearly complete—did he actually compare crucifixions by all three painters, and that was, as he says, to make a joke. He had been discussing El Greco's *Ascension* and then moved on to his *Crucifixion*: "In the far simpler *Crucifixion* we have the purest deed of the man. In this picture the man excels the painter who was never sufficient to himself and he erected for himself a monument which, like all great monuments, can become accessible to everybody.

"By way of a joke I send you a photograph of the *Christ* by Velasquez and the *Christ* by Goya. When I think that there are people who prefer the academic charlatanism of Velasquez and, if they do that, they have no reason for not revering this stuffed noodle by Goya" (Meier-Graefe, 311).

Hemingway will try to outdo Meier-Graefe even when it comes to making jokes about crucifixions and saying unkind things about his admired Goya. He is using the art historian for his own purposes here, much as Huxley used Hemingway. We should also note that Meier-Graefe's book, which is very personal and informal, includes a number of entries on bullfights, which first horrified and then fascinated him. The introduction of him here is rhetorically useful to Hemingway, but it may also be a way of acknowledging and concealing a debt to the art historian for stimulating his thinking about a book on Spain in which bullfighting is treated in the language of art. But Meier-Graefe, despite his central position in this passage, is not Hemingway's main antagonist here. Huxley is. Hemingway's intent in this passage, we believe, is to provide something plainer, earthier, and more direct than Huxley's fanciful and pretentious speculations, and even to answer Huxley's question by showing that what Huxley took as metaphors could be read more literally as having a basis in human sexuality. But let us continue looking at Hemingway's discussion of painting, in which he charged Meier-Graefe with basing his comparative evaluation on a study of crucifixions by the three artists:

> Now it would be hard to do anything stupider than this because of the three only Greco believed in Our Lord or took any interest in his crucifixion. You can only judge a painter by the way he paints the things he believes in or cares for and the things he hates; and to judge Velasquez, who believed in costume, and in the importance of painting as painting, by a portrait of a nearly naked man on a cross who had been painted, Velasquez must have felt, very satis-factorily in the same position before, and in whom Velasquez took no interest at all, is not intelligent.
>
> Goya was like Stendhal; the sight of a priest could stimulate either of those good anti-clericals into a rage of production. Goya's crucifixion is a cynically romantic, wooden oleograph that could serve as a poster for the announcement of crucifixions in the manner of bullfight posters. A crucifixion of six carefully selected Christs will take place at five o'clock in the Monumental Gol-gotha of Madrid, government permission having been obtained. The following well-known, accredited and notable crucifiers will officiate, each accompanied by his cuadrilla of nailers, hammer-ers, cross-raisers and spade-men, etc. (*DIA*, 203–4)

We can make a number of observations about these two paragraphs. Of the painters under consideration, Hemingway's own greatest affinity was undoubtedly with Goya. In his choice of subject matter and in his technique Goya was a master for whom he had the greatest respect. Velasquez, who cared about painting as painting and about costume, as Hemingway put it, is not so close to Hemingway as Goya, but close enough to get respectful if brief attention here. El Greco was the farthest from Hemingway in nearly every respect. Given all this, the obvious thing to do with Meier-Graefe would be to reverse the value judgments attributed to him and single out Goya for praise. But Hemingway has taken a different line. He thinks it foolish to oppose the work of powerful artists to one another because they cared about different things and worked in different styles. He is determined to give each artist his due. He gives El Greco the major part of his interest here, we believe, for two reasons. One is that Huxley's "Meditation on El Greco" is the major motivation of this part of *Death in the Afternoon*. The other reason is that his way of understanding El Greco connected the painter to a theme of considerable importance in this book about bullfighting and in the larger Hemingway Text: the theme of homosexuality.

Hemingway arrives at that theme in the following passage: "Greco liked to paint religious pictures because he was very evidently religious and because his incomparable art was not then limited to accurate reproducing of the faces of the noblemen who were his sitters for portraits and he could go as far into his other world as he wanted and, consciously or unconsciously, paint saints, apostles, Christs and Virgins with the androgynous faces and forms that filled his imagination" (204). In a writer who is often thought of as an archrealist, a writer obsessed with the true gen and the accurate representation of his own place and time, it is at least mildly astonishing to find this impassioned defense of a painter who chafed at the limitations of accurate reproduction and moved repeatedly into his other world of representation. It is also mildly astonishing to find Hemingway—a writer who often resisted or rejected Freudian readings of his own work—casually noting the appropriateness of reading the texts of a painter for thematic material that may have been deployed consciously or unconsciously. And, finally, it is more than mildly astonishing to find Ernest Hemingway, in 1931 or 1932, drawing attention to the androgynous forms that filled El Greco's imagination. But there is more: after calling attention to El Greco's predilection for androgynous forms, Hemingway proceeds to tell the Old Lady about a conversation he had with a writer who was just finishing a book on El Greco. He asked her, "Do you make him a maricón?" When she said, "Why should I?" he continued in this vein: "Did you ever look at the pictures? . . . Did you ever see more classic examples anywhere than he painted? Do you think that was all accident or do you think all those citizens were queer? The only saint I know who is universally represented as built that way is San Sebastian. Greco made them all that way. Look at the pictures" (204).

Writing in this fashion, Hemingway joined the ranks of those he mocked in the glossary, those who find Shakespeare and Leonardo to be "fags." To be sure, he was talking about El Greco rather than Shakespeare or Leonardo, but many would say of the other two that you need only "look at the texts." The point, however, is that Hemingway reasoned from the androgynous images produced by a painter to the painter's sexuality. In the manuscript he also made two interesting changes, writing the word *maricón* over the partially erased word *homosexual* and crossing out the word *fairies* to substitute *classic examples*—alterations in tone rather than substance (K50, 4). We should also remark on how readily Hemingway noted that images of Saint Sebastian are regularly androgynous, an observation confirmed by the current status of that saint as something of a gay icon. Hemingway's argument, though couched in bold and simple prose that keeps affirming a macho subjectivity behind it, is neither trite nor trivial. Here is the concluding paragraph of the chapter:

Velasquez believed in painting, in costume, in dogs, in dwarfs, and in painting again. Goya did not believe in costume but he did believe in blacks and grays, in dust and light, in high places rising from plains, in the country around Madrid, in movement, in his own cojones, in painting, in etching, and in what he had seen, felt, touched, handled, smelled, enjoyed, drunk, mounted, suffered, spewed-up, lain-with, suspected, observed, loved, hated, lusted, feared, detested, admired, loathed, and destroyed. Naturally no painter has been able to paint all that but he tried. El Greco believed in the city of Toledo, in its location and construction, in some of the people who lived in it, in blues, grays, greens and yellows, in reds, in the holy ghost, in the communion and fellow-ship of saints, in painting, in life after death and death after life and in fairies. If he was one he should redeem, for the tribe, the prissy exhibitionistic, aunt-like withered old maid moral arro-gance of a Gide; the lazy, conceited debauchery of a Wilde who betrayed a generation; the nasty, sentimental pawing of humanity of a Whitman and all the mincing gentry. Viva El Greco El Rey de los Maricónes [*sic*]. (204–5)

This is a peroration in which a few rhetorical stops are let out. Emotion, for Hemingway, is frequently expressed in lists deployed in long para-tactic sentences, such as we have here. Among other things, he is letting us know that he has followed his own advice—that he has looked at some pictures so that he can speak of them with emotional conviction and in terms of contrasts and specificities that have a powerfully persua-sive effect. He is also carefully maintaining his own distance from the mincing gentry while singing the praises of the King of the Maricones. His hostile words about Gide, Wilde, and even Whitman are not pre-sented as blanket condemnations of their homosexuality (and it is interesting that he takes Whitman's for granted at a time when many would have denied it fiercely) but in terms of specific attitudes and behaviors.

The most intriguing of the condemnations is that of Wilde. One would like to know what Hemingway had in mind as Wilde's betrayal of a generation. Did he mean that by provoking his own legal difficulties Wilde made it harder for other homosexuals? Or that by writing the saccharine prose and verse of *De Profundis* and *The Ballad of Reading Gaol* he betrayed the wit and irony of his earlier work? These are real questions, but we have no easy answers for them. In the manuscript he had written "betrayed a generation and himself"—which might tilt the interpretive balance toward reading this as a condemnation of Wilde's having come out of the closet so disastrously (K50, 7). In any case, what unites the three objects of Hemingway's scorn in this passage is clearly not the mode of sexuality that links them to El Greco but a way of textualizing that sexuality that allies it with the sentimental and moral-istic: moral arrogance, conceited debauchery, and sentimental pawing of humanity. El Greco, "if he was one" (and we should notice the qualification), redeems all the others. Why? Because of his incompar-able art (204), because he painted what he believed in and because he believed in painting. Also, apparently, because he was not conceited or morally arrogant or one who fawned on humanity.

There are three other places in the book where the subject of homo-sexuality is overtly introduced. The first occasion is quite brief. In chapter 7 the author introduces the topic of the "decadence" of bull-fighting as an art, which in turn leads to a conversation with the Old Lady about this word and its uses and abuses. When the Old Lady objects to all "this discussion of words," the author replies that writers, once they get on that topic, tend to go on and on. "Can you not stop then, sir?" she asks. He responds with a story of "the late Raymond

Radiguet," who made his career "not only with his pen but with his pencil if you follow me" (71). She does indeed follow him, whereupon he relates the following anecdote: "When the late Radiguet was alive he often wearied of the tenuous, rapturous and querulous society of his literary protector, Jean Cocteau, and spent the nights at an hotel near the Luxembourg Gardens with one of two sisters who were then working as models in the quarter. His protector was greatly upset and denounced this as decadence saying, bitterly, yet proudly of the late Radiguet, 'Bebé [*sic*] est vicieuse—il aime les femmes.' So you see, madame, we must be careful chucking the term decadence about since it cannot mean the same to all who read it" (71).

On this occasion Cocteau is treated much as Gide and the other writers will be treated in the later discussion of El Greco, but Radiguet's bisexuality is not. This is the first mention of homosexuality in the book, and it functions as the musical announcement of a theme that will be developed in the text. It enters with apparent "naturalness" in terms of a discussion of "decadence," but there is a twist, since in the illustration the term decadence is attributed to Cocteau, who is said to have used it of Radiguet's lapses into heterosexuality, implying homosexuality as the classic norm from which Radiguet had deviated. Hemingway introduced the term earlier in the chapter in describing contemporary bullfighting, and, when pressed by the Old Lady, he produced a cogent formal definition—"the decay of a complete art through a magnification of certain of its aspects" (70)—before introducing the anecdote. This definition might well have been brought to bear on the work of El Greco, but the point is that Hemingway knew perfectly well how to use the term formally and chose not to apply it to El Greco. Indeed, he called it seriously into question through the anecdote of Cocteau and Radiguet.

But Hemingway's notion of decadence in bullfighting needs to be more closely connected with his interest in homosexual bullfighters. In his definition of the word *maricón* Hemingway gave as his examples one matador of exaggerated delicacy and one of excessive courage. These extremes, as it turns out, are the signs of the decadence of the art of bullfighting. Moreover, it is these extremes and that decadence that provide the focus for Hemingway's interest in the art. He is a professed classicist who is fascinated by decadence—and a professing heterosexual male who is fascinated by maleness that includes too much femaleness, as well as by maleness that is excessively male. Among the bullfighters he found himself in a paradise of sexual excesses and decadence. The topics of homosexuality and decadence are so prevalent in *Death in the Afternoon* that Hemingway finds it easy to stray far from the bullring as long as he sticks to these other interests.

Thus at the end of chapter 15 he manages to introduce the topic of homosexuality in a context far removed from bulls and Spain. And the manner of its introduction is worth noting, both for its content and for its structure, which provides the pattern that will be used for the discussion of El Greco in chapter 17. The leading question (asked by the Old Lady) that allows Hemingway to tell a story about homosexuality in Paris is this one: "Do you know any of the kind of stories Mr. Faulkner writes?" (179). The mention of Faulkner's name here, like the mention of Huxley's in the Greco discussion, was prepared for by a brief discussion of his work in the previous chapter.

Chapter 14 had concluded with the author telling the Old Lady that he plans to spend less time with the bulls and more on writing because "my operatives tell me that through the fine work of Mr. William Faulkner publishers now will publish anything rather than try to get you to delete the better portions of your works, and I look forward to writing of those days of my youth which were spent in the finest whorehouses in the land amid the brilliant society there found" (173). The author is reaffirming his heterosexual credentials (like Radiguet, *il aime les femmes)* and taking an envious jab or two at the author of the recently published *Sanctuary,* who is "prolific" and "writes admirably" of whorehouses: "He writes the best of them of any writer I have read for years." This bit of sparring with Faulkner, who, it is strongly implied, may be writing a bit too rapidly, is a kind of male bonding for which the whorehouse is the medium. There is nothing too surprising in this, but when Faulkner's name comes up later, things are different.

In the next chapter, the Old Lady's innocent inquiry—"Do you know any of the kind of stories Mr. Faulkner writes?"—leads not to a story of prostitution but to one of quite a different sort. The author answers that he knows a few stories but that "told baldly they might not please you" (179). One implication of this is that Faulkner's own stories are never told baldly, suggesting that they are more dependent on their manner than their matter. In the Hemingway Text, however, baldness must be situated as the opposite of an excessive length of hair, in a binary contrast in which gender and sexuality are regularly implicated. In a man, excessive length of hair may call his gender into question. The conversation continues:

> **Old Lady**: Then do not tell them too baldly.
> Madame I will tell you a couple and see how short and how far from bald I can make them. What sort of story would you like first?
> **Old Lady**: Do you know any true stories about those unfortunate people?
> A few, but in general they lack drama as do all tales of abnormality since no one can predict what will happen in the normal while all tales of the abnormal end much the same.
> **Old Lady**: Just the same I would like to hear one. I have been reading of these unfortunate people lately and they are very interesting to me. (179–80)

There is no immediate referent in the text for those unfortunate people, but, as the conversation proceeds, they turn out to be male homosexuals, "abnormals" of whom the author is thus "forced" to speak by the Old Lady's request. With apparent reluctance, then, Hemingway agrees to narrate a tale that will be "tragic enough, but I will not try to write it but only to tell it quickly" (180). He is of course actually writing this story (in fact he wrote it and added it to the typed manuscript of this chapter on the use of the cape after the bullfighting part of the chapter was complete), but he feels compelled to protest that he is only telling it. All this protesting, however, conceals the fact that he had already written, presumably of his own free will, the very story that he is now going to tell.

The earlier written version is called "There's One in Every Town" and runs to eight manuscript pages (K743). The version in *Death in the Afternoon* is indeed abbreviated and includes some other interesting changes, but it is essentially the same story. In both cases, however, a secondary narrator is introduced as the teller of the tale, with the Hemingway figure appearing as a listener and mere recounter of events already recounted by another person who was directly involved. Aesthetically speaking, both versions seek the authenticity of eyewitness narration and the distance obtained by thickening the layers of narrators between the events and the reader. In *Death in the Afternoon* the story is supposed to have been told to the author by "a poor newspaperman, a fool, a friend of mine, and a garrulous and dull companion" (180), who had been awakened the previous night by a commotion in the hotel room next to his and a knock at his door. The knocker was a young man who had arrived with his friend in Paris on that day's boat train. The young man had met his companion, who was a little older, only recently, but they had become great friends, and he had accepted his friend's invitation to come abroad as his guest. His companion had plenty of money and he had none, and their friendship had been a fine and beautiful one until tonight. Now everything was ruined for him (180).

The young man swore that nothing on earth would induce him to go back into that room. At this point the friend knocked on the door and joined the discussion, saying that the first man was "overwrought from the trip." The newspaperman gave them a drink, and the second young man, with "some very sensible reassuring pleading," persuaded the first to rejoin him. The simple newspaperman advised them "to cut it all out and get some sleep" (181). A bit later he was awakened by something that "sounded like fighting in the next room and someone saying, 'I didn't know it was that. . . . I won't! I won't!' followed by what the newspaperman described as a despairing scream" (181). The tale ends with the newspaperman pointing out the two young men to our author, who claims to have seen them frequently afterward on the terrace of the Café des Deux Magots. The last time he saw them, he says, "the younger of the two, the one who said he would kill himself rather than go back into that room, had had his hair hennaed" (182).

This is, then, a tale of recruitment into homosexuality in which a rich and slightly older man uses his economic and physical superiority to force a weaker one into a pattern of life that he later seems to have accepted. In this version, complete with sounds of fighting and that single despairing scream, there is a strong implication that an act of forced anal intercourse has done the trick. The story has been narrated, however, not baldly but with many veils and detours; it treats the reader like a bull who seeks the body of his tormentor, the narrator of the text in which he is implicated, but finds only the cape. This is a chapter on the cape, let us remember. We may assume that the delicacy of this presentation is also meant to contrast with Faulkner's narration of corncob copulation in *Sanctuary*.

The manuscript of the earlier version includes two false starts and one complete draft (K743). The complete draft is presented as an oral recounting of an actual adventure by the person who has encountered the two young men. In this case, however, the narrator is a woman. She seems to be talking to a person who has expressed an interest in seeing specimens of gay Paris. That is, just as in the *Death in the Afternoon* version, the person who tells the story is supposed to be doing so not out of any special interest in the topic but in response to someone else's prurience. The author, it would seem, needs to play both the role of the reluctant narrator and that of the curious spectator while pretending to be neither. "There's One in Every Town" is a monologue that begins, "Oh that's what you want to see is it? Well you can see all of them you want right here" (K743, 1).

The reader, forced into the position of the "you" who wants to see gay Americans in Paris, will get a whole theory of how homosexuals are made in Paris, as well as the narrative of an event much like the one described in *Death in the Afternoon:* "Most of them left some girl behind. Usually she's the librarian or the English teacher in the High School. You know the pretty English teacher. The one that's pretty and brilliant and from such a good family. There's one in every town. And after he's gone away she'll blame it on Paris and him going around and meeting Gertrude Stein and all the literary people. . . . I haven't got anything against them, though. None of them ever left me. I'm not the type: I'm more the Rubens type" (1–2). Gertrude Stein, homosexuality, and painting form a linked cluster in the Hemingway Text, a cluster that includes bullfighting, for it was Stein who introduced Hemingway to both painting and bullfighting, and with whom he talked about male and female homosexuality as well. It is perhaps Stein, then, who has blazed this textual trail connecting the arts of painting and bullfighting with homoeroticism. The female narrator of "There's One in Every

Town," however, presents herself as heterosexual. Nevertheless, she has a fund of true gen about male homosexuality, as well as the particular anecdote that she recounts. From this fund of knowledge she informs her eager listener that young men come to her cafe before they have determined their own sexual orientation and then, again, after they have come out, when it is still exciting for them "just to be known." She can always tell, she adds, by the shape of their faces, the way they walk, and their usual stinginess, telling her interlocutor, who is apparently taking notes, "Put that down. What are you going to do? Write an article about them?" (K743).

The information provided by our Rubensesque narrator is partly confirmed by Hemingway's definition of maricón—and partly contradicted, because one of the exemplary bullfighters of the definition is tight with money and called an "exterior decorator" while the other is clumsy and incapable of saving. The point is that the Hemingway Text feeds on clichés in this area as in others, but it works by both incorporating and contradicting those standard bits of information. In "There's One in Every Town" the narrator, like "Hemingway" in *Death in the Afternoon*, protests that what she has to recount "isn't much of a story" (3). She then goes on to tell much the same story as the one in *Death in the Afternoon*, except that this is a longer version, with dialogue, and it contains an episode that could not be used in the version attributed to a man. In "There's One in Every Town," the narrator has an adjoining room to that of the two young men, and she opens the door in response to knocking and pleading from the other side. After telling the aggressor that this hotel is "no punk house" (a sentence added to the manuscript), she locks him out and invites the other, whom she calls "baby," into her bed. He declines and decides to return to his room and his fate: " 'Kiss me good night,' I said. He did. Just like a girl. I swear I thought I was getting that way myself" (5–6).

This material obviously was recycled in *Death in the Afternoon*. For our purposes, however, a few points are important. One is that this topic keeps returning in the Hemingway Text with an insistence that is notable if not obsessive. Another is that Hemingway uses the expression *punk* to refer to male homosexuals ("This isn't a punk house"). A third is that the female narrator's fear that she may be "getting that way" introduces a theme of transformation by association that appears in such other places in the Hemingway Text as "The Sea Change," in which a man whose woman is leaving him for another woman wants to drink "what the punks drink." A final and perhaps more subtle point is that this female narrator, who is certainly a figure of fun to some degree, also spouts ideas and concerns articulated by Hemingway in his own narrative voice on other occasions, so that these ideas are both presented and withdrawn or undercut at the same time. This ability to enter subject positions quite different from his own and to distance himself from his own views with mockery is one of Hemingway's strong qualities as a writer, and one for which he is rarely given sufficient credit.

Initiation into homosexuality dominates a published Hemingway story as well. The story is "A Simple Enquiry," which appeared in *Men Without Women*, as well it might, since it has an all-male cast. It is a very short tale about an Italian major who discreetly asks his orderly some questions about love and girls to determine whether the orderly might respond to a homosexual advance. When the orderly's replies are discouraging, the major gently dismisses him, still wondering whether or not the orderly is gay: "The little devil, he thought. I wonder if he lied to me" (*CSS*, 252). The major, who has been burnt by the sun in the snowy mountains, has put oil on his burns, leaving him with a "long, burned, oiled face" (251). The orderly, too, is "dark-faced" (a change from the manuscript reading of "with a weak face" [K694, 2]), and after the enquiry is made his face is "flushed" and he "moved differently" (a change from "moved more awkwardly" [K694, 4]) from how "he had moved when he brought in the wood for the fire" (*CSS*, 252). It is this new walk, which the major hears from the other room, that triggers his final musing about whether the orderly lied to him.

As in "There's One in Every Town" the issue here is whether or not one can tell, but in this case the one who cannot tell is himself one of "them." He is presented as a decent man who does not abuse his rank: " 'Don't be afraid,' the major said. His hands were folded on the blankets. 'I won't touch you. You can go back to your platoon if you like. But you had better stay on as my servant. You've less chance of being killed' " (252). The story of this Italian officer is perhaps intended as a deliberate contrast to D. H. Lawrence's "The Prussian Officer," in which the officer abuses and causes the death of his orderly, but we should also read it in terms of its connection to the Hemingway narratives we have just been considering and to others in which the issue of homosocial desire plays a part.

Tanning, as we have seen, is especially linked with transgressive sexuality in the Hemingway Text, and long faces, like those of the figures in El Greco's paintings, are often presented by Hemingway as readable signs of homosexuality. In the present case, however, the major is not presented as especially effeminate or stigmatized in any other way. The story is presented mainly from his point of view, and the irony of the title is that neither the enquiry nor the response is at all simple. In fact, the cliché that it takes one to know one is specifically denied in this story, since the major himself is left wondering at the end. This is a story that parallels in important ways the tale of homosexual initiation presented in "There's One in Every Town" and in chapter 15 of *Death in the Afternoon*. An older man in a position of power seeks to initiate or convert a younger one to the ways of homosexuality. But in this case a simple no suffices—for the moment at least, the question of the future being left open as something that neither the major nor the orderly can be certain about. The change in the orderly's walk can be read in many ways, one of which might be that it is the outward sign of the orderly's discovery of who and what he is. What this story and its Parisian counterparts reveal is the strength of Hemingway's interest in the possibilities of changes in sexual orientation or the revelation of repressed inclinations as they are representable by narratives that focus on moments of initiation or discovery. It is this context that gives a story of negative transformation like "A Simple Enquiry" its resonance.

Redirecting our attention to *Death in the Afternoon,* let us sum up what we have considered so far. In addition to the glossary definition of maricón we have considered three passages that direct our attention to male homosexuality: the anecdote about Cocteau and Radiguet in chapter 6, the story of the homosexual initiation of Americans in Paris in chapter 15, and the discussion of El Greco's androgynous art in chapter 17. In chapter 20, the last chapter of the main text, there are two additional items that seem so brief and elusive that it is quite possible for a reader not to notice them at all. Like the gay Paris anecdote, however, both are traces of larger texts that Hemingway wrote but never developed to a point where he wished to publish them as they were. One of these items is a fleeting mention of "the fairy marquis" who "came out in his car with the boxer" (271), and the other is a fuller reference to actual people Hemingway tried to write about—unsuccessfully in his judgment. Writing of Pamplona, he notes that "they tore down the old Gayarre and spoiled the square to cut a wide thoroughfare to the ring and in the old days there was Chicuelo's uncle sitting drunk in the upstairs dining room watching the dancing in the square; Chicuelo was in his room alone, and the cuadrilla in the café and around the town. I wrote a story about it called *A Lack of Passion,* but it was not good enough although when they threw the dead cats at the train and afterwards the wheels clicking and Chicuelo in the berth, alone; able to do it alone; it was fair enough" (273). The fairy marquis and his boxer might be taken for a dainty nobleman and his dog, but the boxer is a prizefighter and the marquis a maricón. They appear in a long sketch that in its manuscript form is called "Portrait of Three or the Paella" (K660). The title is ambiguous, but one probable reading is that the story is a portrait of three bullfighters and another is that it is a portrait of three maricones, the marquis being one and the other two being bullfighters.

In this narrative Ernesto and three bullfighters (Paco/Aldeano, Paco/Curro, and Sidney [Franklin]) leave the city for a swim in a nearby river. They all strip, enjoy the water, and cook a paella, the recipe for which is provided with the loving care we have come to associate with Julia Child. While they are engaged in these activities the Marqués appears. He is a young man who comes downstream, gazes longingly at the naked quartet, who do not return his gaze, and splashes back, looking over his shoulder all the while. The bullfighters tell the narrator that the man is a "queen" who "comes every day to the river to see what he can fish. . . . And if you look back at him he will say how strong and brown everyone is" (K660, 6). But the young "queen" is not the only one interested in those strong brown bodies. After they all have stripped (and before the Marqués comes fishing), Ernesto describes the bodies of the two Spanish bullfighters in loving detail. The first Paco, later called Curro Prieto in the manuscript, is described as tanned with "fine light muscles" and having only one small scar, and that significantly in the small of his back, probably made while he was running from a bull—a matter confirmed by Sidney, who describes him as having "no guts" (K660, 2). This young man closely resembles one of the two maricones of the glossary—and the protagonist of "A Lack of Passion" as well. The other is described as dark, with hairy legs like an animal and a body that is "beautifully muscled but lithe and fine." But this beautiful body is full of horn scars and whorls in the thighs, groin, abdomen, and even the face. He is "as solid, lithe, honorable and brave as though the bulls had never touched him. Yet he was a failure. Not a failure this year but next year" (3).

This second bullfighter closely resembles the other exemplary maricón of the definition. During the narrative it emerges that the first of the two, like his counterpart in the glossary, is extremely careful with money. We do not know about the second one on this score. The text of this narrative ends with the two Spanish bullfighters arguing about the merit of the whorehouses in their hometowns, thus seeking to imply the strength of their heterosexual tendencies—certainly spurious in one of the two cases and possibly in the other. This connection between prostitution and homosexuality is apparently a link in the Hemingway Text, for it appears in a number of unrelated contexts, such as the discussion of Faulkner and the "unfortunate people" we have already considered, and a later story called "The Light of the World." For the moment, however, it is enough to note that beneath the brief mention of the "fairy Marquis" in *Death in the Afternoon* lies this manuscript that pursues much further the connection between bullfighting and homosexuality— as does another story never quite finished by Hemingway. This one underlies the reference to "A Lack of Passion."

The unfinished manuscript fragments of this story have been usefully (and undogmatically) edited by Susan F. Beegel and published in the *Hemingway Review,* from which we will quote hereafter. The story is usually read as one of impotence, but we see it differently. Hemingway himself, in his second thoughts about it in *Death in the Afternoon,* remembers the young bullfighter Chicuelo, in his berth on the railroad train, "alone; able to do it alone" (273). What Chicuelo is able to do alone, here, is clearly erotic. The boy is masturbating. But the available manuscripts do not make this situation quite as explicit as Hemingway remembered it to be. The closest version to his own recollection is the

end of Beegel's "Third Manuscript," which takes place in the compartment of a train and reads this way: "The Uncle shut the door. Gavira
turned his head against the wall. He felt the train moving. A cool breath
of air came through the window" (Beegel, 80). Either there was another
version, now lost, or Hemingway remembered something that he did
not actually write but thought of as having happened. This is by no
means the only case where <u>masturbation</u> may have been on Hemingway's mind but not in his writing, but this case is especially interesting
because we can find only the slightest textual support for this reading.
Many such moments in Hemingway's writing lead us to believe that the
Hemingway Text often extends beyond the words on the page and
requires the active participation of a reader who is not afraid to extrapo-
late from hints.

This is especially important in "A Lack of Passion" because there are
other hints that must be interpreted as well. The story had two other
titles before Hemingway settled on the final one: "Disgrace" and "Chicuelo—The *Phemenomenon*." The second title, which feminizes the
bullfighter by adding an extra syllable to the word *phenomenon* (phem
[fem]-enomenon), interests us here. Chicuelo (or Gavira—Hemingway
jotted down many possible names for this character) is, like one of the
prototypical mariconic toreros, an artist with the cape but a coward. As
the story opens he has just given the worst of a series of disastrous
performances in the bullring—so bad that his promoter uncle is worried
about getting safely out of town. The story is set during the evening after
his last fiasco. In one of the manuscripts a second fiasco occurs—this
one in his hotel room.

In a fragment intended to be added to page 16 of the last (typescript)
version of the story, the hotel maid offers to do a sexual favor for
Gavira. He insists on the light being off and the door locked. From that
point the conversation goes this way:

In the dark he said, "Is that all right?"

"No, like this."

"I don't want it like that."

"Yes. Yes oh please. Oh let me. Let me let me."

In the dark he lay quiet. It wasn't any good. Not that or any other.

"Get out and don't turn the light on."

"No. Please no. Let me."

"Get out you whore."

"And you," she said, "What are you? What are you, matador?"

"Get out," he said.

"Maracón," she said. "Matador, maracón." [The misspellings are corrected in the manuscript.]

"No," said Gavira. "Just nothing. Nothing. Just nothing." (Beegel, 93)

A man and a woman in bed debating how they will or will not do this or that—without the specifics of this or that being provided in the text—is a topic that was to return in the Hemingway Text with a vengeance in *The Garden of Eden*. In the present case, however, and even though he needed to check on the spelling of the word *maricón*, Hemingway clearly wanted the concept of homosexuality introduced in the story. The bullfighter denies the charge, saying he is just a nothing, but another episode in the narrative pushes interpretation again in that direction.

In getting through the crowd and into the bus taking the cuadrilla to the railroad station, Gavira is helped by one of the banderillos, Salas. The other banderillo, Rubito, is a womanizer, often stricken with vene-real disease ("Rubito always had his cock in a sling" [Beegel, 75]). But Salas is "different." He is a "funny one"—crossed out in manuscript (Beegel, 75). "Gavira liked to be with Salas. It meant something to be with him, something definite he always felt. He did not think now being with him" (Beegel, 77). Salas helps Gavira avoid being tripped by his own cuadrilla members as he enters the bus. The first version of the story ends with them sitting opposite each another, knees touching, Gavira "not thinking." In the later typescript, the episode in the bus is developed more fully. Once again Salas protects Gavira from being tripped and they sit opposite one another: "Gavira sat, his knees touching Salas. No one, except the drunken picador, had spoken to him. An electric tram climbing the hill to the town passed them. Gavira was not thinking. He was only sitting there, sitting beside [blank space]. Inside the bus now, riding in the dark he felt quiet and peaceful all through himself. He did not know what it was but the sitting there made it all quiet. Salas did not touch him. It was just the pressure of his knees against him crowded in the bus. It was not a pressure. It was just that they touched him. Salas put his hand on Gavira's knee in the dark and let it rest there" (Beegel, 90). Chicuelo was the nickname of a real bullfighter, Manuel Jiminez, whom Hemingway described this way in chapter 8 of *Death in the Afternoon:* "Chicuelo was the son of a matador of that same name who had been dead some years from tuberculosis. He was reared, trained and launched and managed by his uncle Zocato, who had been a banderillo of the old school and was a good business man and a heavy drinker. Chicuelo was short, unhealthily plump, without a chin, with a bad complexion, tiny hands, and the eyelashes of a girl. Trained in Sevilla and then on the ranches around Salamanca he was as perfect a miniature bullfighter as could be manufactured and he was about as authentic a bullfighter, really, as a little porcelain statuette" (73–74).

There can be little doubt that the fictional Gavira took shape as an imaginative version of the real Chicuelo and that the development of this imaginary figure led to positioning him as a youth in search of a pederast. He is, then, another version of the young man about to be initiated into homosexuality of "There's One in Every Town." Like that

Parisian manuscript, this Spanish one even includes the opportunity for sex with a woman in a hotel room. But this is not the same story, even though it is an adaptation of the pattern. Hemingway was interested in how sexuality got defined and how it changed, and he was especially interested the alternatives to "normal" sexual patterns. Contrary to his own statement about the sameness of abnormality, his stories show that there are so many varieties of normal and abnormal that the whole distinction is threatened by them. If "There's One in Every Town" showed us the making of American homosexuals in Paris, and "A Simple Enquiry" showed a moment of hesitation or rejection of a homosexual overture in Italy, "A Lack of Passion" shows us a Spanish Infanta on the verge of becoming a Queen. It also offers us in the character of Salas— and this portrait is sketched very delicately—a man who is tender and protective of another man, a man who is "different" and does not chase women, and who is also strong and courageous himself. The instances of homoeroticism in the Hemingway Text are not only many, they are also various and subtle.

One that appears less subtle, however, is the published story "Mother of a Queen," which is about a Mexican matador who is one of the stingy maricones, so tight that he will not pay twenty dollars to keep his mother's remains from being removed from her grave and "dumped on the common bone heap" (*CSS*, 316). Told from the point of view of someone in the matador's cuadrilla, the story ends with the narrator trying to insult the matador by saying to him, "You never had a mother," which is supposed to be the worst insult possible in Spanish, but the matador turns it away, saying, "That's true. . . . My poor mother died when I was so young it seems as though I never had a mother" (319). The tale ends with the narrator muttering about the difficulty of insulting a man who won't respond in the manly way.

This story seems blunt enough to refute our claims about the subtlety of Hemingway's presentation of a range of sexual attitudes and behaviors. In the Hemingway Text, however, every individual work must be read in the context of others linked to it thematically and formally. "Mother of a Queen" must be read in the context of a companion story that has not, unfortunately, been published. We say unfortunately not because this is a lost masterpiece but because it presents a side of Hemingway that is often ignored and, for many readers, scarcely imaginable. It is also a very funny story. Like "Mother of a Queen" it is set in Mexico and may have been drawn from the repertory of tales told to Hemingway by the American bullfighter Sidney Franklin ("one of the best story tellers I have ever heard" *(DIA,* 475), who fought in Mexico for some years and also appeared as a character in "Portrait of Three." It lacks a title but we will call it for purposes of reference "A Real Man." Like "Mother of a Queen" it is told by a member of a matador's cuadrilla and leads to the same key phrase, the deadly Spanish insult charging the insulted with the lack of a mother.

"A Real Man" (K831) begins where "A Lack of Passion" ended, in a train compartment. Only in this case the narrator is in the upper berth and the matador he works for is in the lower. In the middle of the night the narrator is awakened and asked to admire his boss' enormous erection: "Mister, look. Isn't it a wonder?" "I'd look," the narrator tells us, "and it would nearly reach to the top of the berth and I'd laugh and go back to sleep" (1). But the matador is not satisfied with being looked at just once and wakes the narrator a second time. In the manuscript narration of this second gaze there is a spelling slip that takes us all the way back to "Indian Camp," but that is not what is most important here: "I would put my head around over the side of the birth [*sic*] and there he would be lying with the berth light on his pockmarked face, with the hair down on his forehead and his pyjama jacket open so you could see the scar two inches wide that ran across his chest and that damned thing sticking up like a baseball bat." The narrator urges the matador to masturbate and go to sleep, but the man is too much in love with his erection to do anything about it. He wants to make sure it is seen. "You see it?" he says. And the narrator answers, "See it. Is there any time I don't see[k—crossed out] it? It hangs half way down to your knee in the traje de luces" (K831, 2). If we think of poor Chicuelo in his berth "alone, able to do it alone," as Hemingway remembered the ending of "A Lack of Passion," here we have another figure in a berth— only this one is *un*able to do it alone because he so admires his own penis as a visible object. He is also, it happens, no luckier with women than Chicuelo. The only time we see him with a woman he reaches for a girl sitting near him in a cantina, grabbing her so roughly that he hurts her, and she screams. When he asks her to go upstairs with him she says, "No. . . . You're just an animal." He replies that he is a man, "a man such as you have never seen" (4). This bullfighter is so macho and so narcissistic that he turns himself into an object of the gaze, so much a man that he feminizes himself. As the narrator reports, he has a nasty habit of getting drunk in cantinas and taking out his beautiful object, laying it on the bar, and asking the patrons "to have a drink to it" (3). Yes, this is Ernest Hemingway satirizing the macho excesses of a very virile bull-fighter. As a companion piece to "Mother of a Queen" this little tale also turns on the Spanish insult to maternity that so fascinated Hemingway. When no woman at his table will go upstairs with him he switches from sexual mode to fighting mode and insults the entire town: "You've never seen a man," he said. "There's not a man in this stinking little town." He looked around. "Nor in this cantina." He stood up. "Nor has any man in this cantina a mother" (K831, 5).

The matador in "Mother of a Queen" refused to hear that very insult. This matador insults a whole cantina full of men who also refuse to hear it. In a matador, in a man, the extremes of effeminacy and hypermasculinity are equally fascinating and equally repellent. And both paths lead to an intense narcissism that separates the individual from contact with other humans. In this respect, as in others, it could be argued that the macho savage, the male as animal, is the object of a greater satiric force than the queen of the other story, but our point is that the tales belong together, that they should be read and studied together, and that they both delineate extremes of male behavior that are coded as offensive or ridiculous in the Hemingway Text. They also should help us to attend more closely to those representations of homosocial desire in the Hemingway Text that are positioned between the extremes presented in these two satiric tales.

One such narrative is "The Undefeated," a bullfighting story widely regarded as one of Hemingway's major works of short fiction. There is a case to be made for pairing "The Undefeated" with "A Lack of Passion" in the same way we paired "Mother of a Queen" with "A Real Man," for "The Undefeated" is about a penniless, clumsy, and very brave bullfighter. That is, the hero—and he is a hero—of the story conforms perfectly to the characteristics of one of the maricones described in the glossary and to Paco/Aldeano in "Portrait of Three," just as Chicuelo conforms to the other glossary maricón and to Paco/Churro in "Portrait of Three." There is no revelation of Manuel Garcia's sexuality in "The Undefeated," which is about a man's relationship to another man and to his ideal image of himself. But Manuel Garcia and "Manos" Zurito are both "Men Without Women." Their relationship does not have the more overt sexuality of "A Lack of Passion," but it is nonetheless like that of Salas and Gavira (or Chicuelo), for Zurito (a picador as Salas was a banderillo) is older, stronger, and protective of the torero he serves.

As a narrative, "The Undefeated" turns upon the possibility that Garcia will allow his *coleta* (pigtail) to be cut off; the pigtail is the symbol of his status as a matador ("once the caste mark of all bullfight-ers," the glossary says). This is, then, like "A Real Man," another story of a bullfighter and his phallic symbol, only in this case Garcia's man-hood is not mocked—but it is not simply celebrated either. Zurito, who has come out of retirement to pic for Garcia, has obtained a promise that if things go badly again, Garcia will allow his coleta to be cut off. But at the end, with the scarred body of the gored Garcia on the operating table once more and Zurito poised with the scissors for another kind of operation, Garcia pleads, "You couldn't do a thing like that, Manos" (*CSS*, 204). Zurito replies, "I won't do it. I was joking," and the story ends with him standing "awkwardly, watching" as the other operation begins (205).

This story needs to be read against its opposite, "A Lack of Passion," and against its parody, which we have called "A Real Man." In "A Real Man" an actual penis becomes such a phallic symbol as to be a joke, and the narrator predicts that somebody will cut it off some day. In "The Undefeated" a phallic symbol becomes a part of the body that it would be fatal to remove. Any deconstructive critic could imagine such opposi-tions for a major text like "The Undefeated," but it is important for us as readers to know that Hemingway himself not only imagined but wrote them and preserved them as a part of the Hemingway Text. Our conten-tion is that the Hemingway who did these things is a more interesting writer than the Hemingway seen as the advocate and the embodiment of a mindless machismo. Both of these Hemingways are fictions, of course, though both are connected to what we know of the life of the man, which leaves us with two interesting questions: Which is the more plausible, and which will most enhance our readings of the Text?

Before concluding this chapter on homosocial desire among boys and men in the Hemingway Text, we must look at one more story that touches on the topic. This story is one of the boxing stories, which often have overtones of homosocial desire. The story in question is called "The Light of the World," and it has proved to be something of a puzzle to critics and readers of Hemingway. In the story two young men come into a bar for a drink, have some kind of altercation with the bartender, and then go down to the railroad station, where there are "six white men and four Indians" (*CSS*, 293). The men are lumbermen, except for the camp cook, who is singled out for verbal abuse as a homosexual. There are also three whores in the station—one of whom is described as an enormous "three hundred and fifty pounds" by the boy narrator—who get involved in a long, confused discussion about their supposed personal relationships with a boxer whose name they have got wrong (though the cook gets it right). The two boys talk to the cook and to the big whore; the cook and the whore also spar verbally with one another. One of the whores says she could have married the boxer but decided not to hurt his career (a parody of Brett's decision in *The Sun Also Rises)*. The narrator is becoming interested in the huge whore, but his friend notices this and calls him away. When the cook asks where they are going, he replies, "The other way from you" (297).

All this is inconsequential enough, apparently. The story is usually read as being narrated by a young Nick Adams, though the narrator has no name in the written text. What is missing in most analyses, however, is attention to the bartender's reaction to the boys and the cause of their altercation. Quite simply, he thinks they are homosexuals: "All you punks stink. . . . You punks clear the hell out of here" (292–93). His attitude toward them is similar to that of the lumbermen toward the cook. Many critics, however, believing that the narrator is Nick who is Ernest Hemingway who is not a maricón, simply cannot see sexual orientation as an issue in the story. As we read it, however, the story is very much about sexual orientation, focusing on the two boys (seventeen and nineteen) who may not, as the narrator of "There's One in

Every Town" says, "know which way they're going to jump" (K743, 1). The bartender may be as wrong in calling them punks as the whore is who almost married "Steve" Ketchel, but the repeated use of the word introduces the theme of homosexuality, which is then carried on by the presentation of the cook and the brutal teasing of his macho companions.

The narrator's friend, Tommy, also teases the cook by answering his question about the boys' ages with "I'm ninety-six and he's sixty-nine," which makes the whores laugh, but the narrator replies, "We're seventeen and nineteen." The narrator does not join in the teasing of the cook, and he begins to find the huge whore attractive: "She had a pretty face and a nice smooth skin and a lovely voice and she was nice all right and really friendly" (297). Like the younger of the two men in "There's One in Every Town," this narrator seems to be poised between two kinds of sexuality—those of the gay cook and the huge hooker, who offers a maternal as well as an erotic image—but his friend takes him away. To what? We just don't know. We don't know whether these boys are actual or possible punks; all we know is that they are situated in a world in which they have only three choices: the cook, the hooker, and one another. As in so many other strong stories by Hemingway, what makes this one interesting is precisely its ambiguity—its sexual ambiguities in particular. But, if we do not pick up on the sexual orientation implied by that word *punk,* we will miss a crucial aspect of the way the problem is being posed. This story belongs with both "There's One in Every Town" and "A Simple Enquiry" as a story about sexuality in the process of formation—a process that may be completed or diverted. Vladimir Nabokov once tossed off a witticism to the effect that Hemingway wrote exclusively about "bulls, balls, and belles," which sounds fine, but bulls, balls, and boys would have been more to the point.

Have we been trying to show that Hemingway was gay? No. If

anything, we have been trying to show that such a question is too simple. The complexity of human sexuality—especially the potential bisexuality of all humans—were issues that had been given a prominent place in the cultural text by Fliess, Freud, and Weininger around the turn of the century. These issues were in the air that Hemingway and other artists of his time were breathing. What we have been trying to show is that Hemingway was much more interested in these matters than has usually been supposed—and much more sensitive and complex in his consideration of them.

Afterword

An afterword, not a conclusion. In examining certain aspects of gender in the Hemingway Text we have hoped to open a conversation rather than close one. Still, it may be useful to look back at the ground we have covered. We began by looking at the word *Papa* and finding it used, in contexts far removed from Hemingway's world, to signify thoughtless propagation, false paternity, and a cry of pain. Following these extravagant lures, we found clues to the anguish and uncertainty concealed beneath the blunt facade of Papa Hemingway—emotions that are powerfully inscribed in important parts of the Hemingway Text. Beneath the patriarchal mask one can discern the features of a man resisting the paternal: an anti-Papa.

From this central question of manliness, briefly considered, we moved to one of Hemingway's major problems as a writer: the representation of female characters, codified by Leslie Fiedler's remark that "there are no women in his books." Starting with Mummies, real and fictional, we tried to show that the many women inscribed in the Hemingway Text can be seen as variants of a basic repertory of female types. In examining a range of Hemingway's fictional women we suggested that his most successful representations be seen as combining features of more than one of his basic types or as taking on attributes of gender commonly coded as male.

In Chapter 3 we pursued this topic more deeply, exploring the ways lesbianism, sex changes, and miscegenation function as centers of interest in Hemingway's early and late writing, reaching a peak of fascination in the manuscript of *The Garden of Eden*—a peak visible even in the heavily censored published version of the novel. In our final chapter we turned from what may be thought of as female figures complicated by maleness to male figures complicated by femaleness. Putting things this way is too simple, of course, if only because Hemingway himself seems to have seen lesbianism and male homosexuality not only as cases in which individuals may be said to combine both genders but also as cases that may be thought of as involving an excess of one gender's attributes, as in the case of the pathetically phallic bullfighter, who has no luck with women and is reduced to exposing himself to other men in bars and challenging them to fight him.

We would be the first to admit that there is more to be done with all of these matters, but we hope that our contribution to the topic will at least make it difficult to think of Hemingway as a writer with too much machismo for his own good—someone, as he put it himself, who had eaten too many criadillas. The Hemingway you were taught about in high school is dead. *Viva el nuevo Hemingway.*

Works Cited

To be as precise as possible about the location of the Hemingway Manuscripts at the John F. Kennedy Library we have used the following system. The letter K followed by a number (with or without a decimal point) identifies the catalogue number. A second number following a slash indicates a folder. Page numbers within folders are identified following a comma. Thus K422.5/4, 12 is Kennedy Library item number 422.5, folder 4, page 12. We are grateful to the Hemingway Foundation for permission to quote from these materials.

Anderson, Sherwood. *Horses and Men*. New York: B. W. Huebsch, 1923.

Barkan, Leonard. *The Gods Made Flesh*. New Haven: Yale University Press, 1986.

Beegel, Susan. " 'A Lack of Passion': Its Background, Sources, and Composition History" and "Hemingway's 'A Lack of Passion' and the 'Lack of Passion' Papers." *Hemingway Review* 9, no. 2 (Spring 1990): 50–93.

Benstock, Shari. *Women of the Left Bank*. Austin: University of Texas Press, 1986.

Bullough, Vern. *Sexual Variance in Society and History*. Chicago: Chicago University Press, 1980.

Comley, Nancy R. "Hemingway's Economics of Survival." *Novel* 12 (Spring 1979): 244–53.

Courtivron, Isabelle de. "Weak Men and Fatal Women: The Sand Image." In *Homosexualities and French Literature*, edited by George Stamboulian and Elaine Marks, 210–227. Ithaca, N.Y.: Cornell University Press, 1979.

Cowley, Malcolm. "A Portrait of Mister Papa." *Life*, 10 January 1949: 86–101.

Fiedler, Leslie. *Love and Death in the American Novel*. New York: Dell, 1969.

Freud, Sigmund. "The Sexual Enlightenment of Children" (1907). In *The Sexual Enlightenment of Children*. New York: Collier, 1969.

Gautier, Théophile. *Mademoiselle de Maupin* (1835). New York: Boni and Liveright, 1918.

Gould, Thomas E. " 'A Tiny Operation with Great Effect': Authorial Revision and Editorial Emasculation in the Manuscript of Hemingway's *For Whom the Bell Tolls*." In *Blowing the Bridge: Essays on Hemingway and "For Whom the Bell Tolls,"* edited by Rena Sanderson, 67–81. New York: Greenwood, 1992.

Hemingway, Ernest. *Across the River and into the Trees.* New York: Scribners, 1971.

———. *The Complete Short Stories of Ernest Hemingway.* Finca Vigía Edition. New York: Scribners, 1987.

———. *Death in the Afternoon.* New York: Scribners, 1960.

———. *A Farewell to Arms.* New York: Scribners, 1929.

———. *The Fifth Column and Four Stories of the Spanish Civil War.* New York: Scribners, 1969.

———. *For Whom the Bell Tolls.* New York: Scribners, 1940.

———. *The Garden of Eden.* New York: Scribners, 1986.

———. *The Garden of Eden* Manuscripts. Hemingway Collection, Kennedy Library, Boston.

———. *The Green Hills of Africa.* New York: Scribners, 1963.

———. *Islands in the Stream.* New York: Scribners, 1970.

———. *A Moveable Feast.* New York: Scribners, 1964.

———. *The Nick Adams Stories.* New York: Scribners, 1972.

———. *Selected Letters.* Edited by Carlos Baker. New York: Scribners, 1981.

———. *The Short Stories of Ernest Hemingway.* New York: Scribners, 1966.

———. *The Sun Also Rises.* New York: Scribners, 1954.

———. *To Have and Have Not.* New York: Scribners, 1937.

Hemingway, Mary Welsh. *How It Was.* New York: Knopf, 1976.

Huxley, Aldous. *Music at Night and Other Essays* (1931). London: Chatto and Windus, 1949.

Judrin, Claudie. *Rodin et les écrivains de son temps.* Paris: Musée Rodin, 1976.

Kert, Bernice. *The Hemingway Women.* New York: Norton, 1983.

Lampert, Catherine. *Rodin: Sculpture and Drawings.* London: Arts Council of Great Britain, 1986.

Lessing, Gotthold Ephraim. *Laocoön.* Translated by E. A. McCormick. Indianapolis: Bobbs-Merrill, 1962.

Lewis, Wyndham. "The Dumb Ox, A Study of Ernest Hemingway." In *Men Without Art,* 19–36. Santa Rosa, Calif.: Black Sparrow Press, 1987.

Lynn, Kenneth. *Hemingway.* New York: Simon and Schuster, 1987.

Meier-Graefe, Julius. *The Spanish Journey.* Translated by J. Holroyd-Reece. New York: Harcourt, Brace, 1930.

Ovid. *The Metamorphoses.* Translated by Rolfe Humphries. Bloomington: Indiana University Press, 1955.

Reynolds, Michael. *Hemingway's First War.* Oxford: Basil Blackwell, 1976.

————. *Hemingway's Reading, 1910–1940.* Princeton: Princeton University Press, 1981.

————. *The Young Hemingway.* Oxford: Basil Blackwell, 1986.

Ross, Lillian. Profile, "How Do You Like It Now, Gentlemen?" *New Yorker,* 13 May 1950, 36–62.

Scholes, Robert. *Semiotics and Interpretation.* New Haven: Yale University Press, 1982.

Sedgwick, Eve Kosofsky. *Between Men: English Literature and Male Homosocial Desire.* New York: Columbia University Press, 1985.

Smith, Paul. *A Reader's Guide to the Short Stories of Ernest Hemingway.* Boston: G. K. Hall, 1989.

Sophocles. *Philoctetes.* Edited by F. P. Graves. Boston: Leach, Shewell, and Sanborn, 1893.

Spilka, Mark. *Hemingway's Quarrel with Androgyny.* Lincoln: University of Nebraska Press, 1989.

Tancock, John. *The Sculpture of Auguste Rodin.* Philadelphia: Philadelphia Musem of Art, 1976.

Theweleit, Klaus. *Male Fantasies.* Vol. 1. Minneapolis: University of Minnesota Press, 1987.

Villard, Henry, and James Nagel. *Hemingway in Love and War.* Boston: Northeastern University Press, 1989.

Weininger, Otto. *Sex and Character.* New York: G. P. Putnam's Sons, 1907.

Wilson, Edmund. *The Wound and the Bow* (1941). New York: Farrar, Straus and Giroux, 1978.

Index